By the Word of Their Testimony

"And they overcame him because of the
blood of the Lamb and because of the
word of their testimony…"
Revelation 12:11

Nothing is Impossible With God

Book 3

Cover Design by Dallas & Tara Thiele • NarrowRoad Publishing House

By the Word of Their Testimony
Nothing is Impossible With God

Published by:
NarrowRoad Publishing House
POB 830
Ozark, MO 65721 U.S.A.

The materials from Restore Ministries were written for the sole purpose of encouraging women. For more information, please take a moment to visit us at: **www.EncouragingWomen.org** or **www.RestsoreMinistries.net.**

Permission from the author has been given to those who wish to print or photocopy this book for themselves or others, strictly for encouragement and informational purposes; however, such copies or reprints cannot be sold in any form without prior written permission from the author.

Unless otherwise indicated, most Scripture verses are taken from the *New American Standard Bible* (NASB). Scripture quotations marked KJV are taken from the *King James Version* of the Bible, and Scripture quotations marked NIV are taken from the *New International Version*. Our ministry is not partial to any particular version of the Bible but **love** them all so that we are able to help every woman in any denomination who needs encouragement and who has a desire to gain greater intimacy with her Savior.

Library of Congress Control number: 2015913039
ISBN: 1-931800-30-8
ISBN 13: 978-1-931800-30-3

Contents

Introduction

Your Divine Appointment

"I was **crying** to the LORD with my voice,
And He **answered me** from His holy mountain"
—Psalm 3:4.

Have you been searching for marriage help? It's not by chance, nor is it by coincidence, that you are reading this book. God has heard your cry for help in your marriage dilemma. He predestined this DIVINE APPOINTMENT to give you the hope that you so desperately need right now!

If you have been told that your marriage is hopeless or that without your spouse's help your marriage cannot be restored, then this is the book you need. Read this over and over so you will begin to believe that God is MORE than able to restore ANY marriage, including YOURS!

We know and understand what you are going through since WE, and MANY others who have come to our ministry for help, have a restored marriage and family! No matter what others have told you, your marriage is NOT hopeless!! We KNOW, after twenty five years of ministry, that God is able to restore ANY marriage, even YOURS!

If you have been crying out to God for more help, someone who understands, then join our Internet Restoration Fellowship Online and you'll receive an ePartner (email partner) who will help you see your marriage through to restoration during your rebuilding phase of your journey. Since beginning this fellowship, we have seen more marriages restored on a regular basis than we ever thought possible!

So, if you are really serious in your desire to restore your marriage, then our fellowship is the answer. For more information or to join, go to our website RMIEW.com. We would love for you to be a part of our Restoration Fellowship!

Who are we and what are we hoping to do?

Restore Ministries helps those who have found themselves in a hopeless situation: couples whose spouse is in adultery, has left, has filed for divorce, or any other seemingly impossible marital situation. These broken people have often sought help, but everyone (many times even their pastors) have told them their marriage was hopeless. However, we not only believe that no marriage is hopeless – regardless of the circumstances—we know they aren't. That's why we offer hope, help and encouragement through our website, our Restoration Fellowship, and a variety of resources including a variety of newsletters to spiritual feed and uplift you daily!

In 2001, Restoration Fellowship was birthed to minister more effectively to the needs of those seriously seeking restoration. Within a year the fellowship grew to over 400 committed members and increases daily with members from all over the world.

Restore Ministries has never sought advertising or paid for placement in search engines but has instead grown by word of mouth. We also take no support from anyone but the individuals themselves who are seeking restoration so that we are never told we must comprise sharing His full truths. Though often ostracized by the established church, because of those who have cried out to God for help when their own church, pastor, family and friends who offered them **no** hope or support, we have given them hope and we have become an oasis in the desert for the desperate, the hurting, the rejected.

Often accused of being extreme, radical, out-of-balance or legalistic, the message in all our resources is founded firmly on the Word of God only, encouraging those seeking restoration to live the message that Jesus proclaimed, beginning with the familiar Beatitudes.

RMI teaches the good news of God's Word to bring healing to the brokenhearted, comfort to those in pain, and freedom to prisoners of despondency and sin through the truth of His Word, giving them the hope that is "against all hope" through the Power of Jesus Christ, the Mighty Counselor and Good Shepherd.

Our site and our resources minister to the hurting all over the world with the intent of creating a deeper and more intimate walk with the Lord that results in the hurting healed, the bound freed, the naked clothed, the lost saved and broken marriages restored. We minister to women from more than 15 countries including Switzerland, Hong Kong, New Zealand, Sweden, Philippines, Brazil and Germany, with large followings in Australia, Canada, and Africa. Our books have been translated into Spanish, Portuguese, Tagalog (Filipino), Afrikaans, and French. Also Slovakian, Chinese, Russian, Italian and some Hindi.

Jesus said that you "will know them by their fruits" that's why this book and all our *By the Word of Their Testimony* books are filled with testimonies of hopeless marriages that were restored, marriages that give glory to God and to the Power of His Word. Our *WOTT* books are growing at such a phenomenal rate that we were once unable to keep up with getting them published. Now we have a full team devoted to keeping up.

If you have any doubt about the validly of our ministry, you won't after reading this and our other awesome books. Each will show you not only hopeless marriages that were restored, but more importantly, it will show you men and women who have been completely transformed into God-lovers and are now committed on-fire Christians, many of whom were saved through this ministry.

Below is a small sampling of the letters of gratitude that Restore Ministries has received. Please note when you read the letters that they give all the praise and glory to the Lord. This ministry was founded and continues to grow on the premise that "if He be lifted up, He will draw all men to Himself" and "the Lord will share His glory with no man."

"Let Another Praise You" Proverbs 27:2

I honestly don't think that anything I can say will reflect how very grateful I am for you. THANK YOU feels insufficient, but from the very bottom of my heart, I really do thank you for this beautiful gift of your books, lessons, and ministry. THANK YOU for allowing God to use you in this way to change so many lives like you changed mine!

When I found RMI my marriage was completely dead and so was I (spiritually). Whilst I am still separated from my husband, I have changed completely. My marriage may still look dead in the physical, but I am standing on my God and His promises, He can and WILL restore my marriage.

Before I found you, I didn't feel as though life was worth living. I just couldn't see anything positive or good in my future, it was just a big black fog. Over the past 30 days, my life has been completely transformed! Not only have I developed a relationship with God that is so real and deep, that I didn't think it was ever possible to know God in such an intimate way; but I am so hungry and on fire for HIM! I seek God firsthand foremost, He is in my every thought and in every thing I do. The more I have drawn closer to Him, He has done the exact same to me, and I just feel completely surrounded and clothed in His love, grace, peace and mercy. The bible is no longer 'a book to read'. It is my life manual that contains all the beautiful promises that my God has made to me. The cross really is before me and the world is thankfully behind me - forever!

The principles helped me, not only during this season of my life, but will guide me forever. I pray that more and more women come to this place of seeking God (and him only), and as a result experience the level of intimacy that God desires. I just have this image of women all over the world, on their knees praising God and allowing Him to mould them and fulfilling the call and purpose his has for their live—thanks to you. It's about time we give the enemy the migraine of all migraines!

Once again, thank you and God bless you and your families...you're all in my prayers.

~ Denna in the United Kingdom

Thank YOU so very much for your everything, which game me the opportunity to renew my mind and heal my heart. I am so grateful, so much that I am able continue to read and reread everything you provide me with. With this said, my heartfelt thanks to ERIN for all the wonderful works, for AWESOME books, —yes I agree with one of the ladies whose marriage is restored that through ERIN, He uses her as a vessel to get to know and be intimate with our Lord Jesus Christ. Praise the Lord! Thank you RMI I have found Him too!! :)

Your resources are the best books I've ever read - I learned the TRUTH in God's Words and reading RYM is an eye opener to me and a wake up call! and it made me closer to our LORD! Studying HIs words give me a PEACE OF MIND and I know HE is always there for us.

Thank You RMI! Again, thank you ERIN!

When I found my way here, there was lot of anger, I felt helpless knowing EH was living with the OW and I had a hard time letting go of him. Now I want to say to everyone reading this Don't Give UP and begin to read HIS Words, the Bible and pray unceasingly. You are about to change!!

~Ally in California

We put this book and all our *Word of Their Testimony* books together because we believe that as you spend some time reading these incredible and awesome testimonies of seemingly hopeless marriages that were miraculously restored, you will be encouraged and know without a doubt...

NOTHING IS IMPOSSIBLE WITH GOD!!

Nothing is Impossible with God!

"Looking at them, Jesus said,
'With people it is impossible,
but not with God;
for all things are possible with God.'"
Mark 10:27

*"And they overcame him because of the blood of the Lamb and because of the **word of THEIR testimony**, and they did not love their life even to death." Rev. 12:11.*

The following testimonies are filled with miracles of men and women who took God at His Word and believed that "nothing was impossible with God!" Those who have had the miracle of a restored marriage have several things in common. All "delighted themselves in the Lord" and He gave them "the desires of their heart." All of them "hoped against hope" when their situation seemed hopeless.

All of them "fought the good fight" and "finished their course." All of them were determined "not to be overcome with evil" but instead to "overcome evil with good." All were willing to "bless their enemies" and to pray for them that "despitefully used and persecuted them." All "turned the other cheek" and "walked the extra mile." All realized that it was "God who removed lover and friend far from" them and it was God who "made them a loathing" to their spouse. All of them understood and believed that it is NOT the will of man (or woman) but the "will of God" who can "turn the heart" whichever way He chooses.

All refused to fight in "the flesh" but chose to battle "in the spirit." None were concerned to protect themselves, but trusted themselves "to Him who judges righteously." All of their trust was "in the Lord" because their trust was "the Lord." All released their attorneys (if that was part of their testing) since they "would rather be wronged or defrauded." All of them "got out of the way of wickedness" and "let the unbeliever leave" since they "were called to peace." All refused to do "evil for evil or insult for insult." All loved their spouse who may have been unfaithful because they knew that "love never fails."

This is the same journey that the Lord took me on back in 1989. That year I made a promise to God that if He would restore my marriage to my husband, I would devote my life to telling others about Him and His desire and ability to restore ANY marriage no matter what the circumstances. The Lord was faithful and restored my marriage, suddenly, two years later after a divorce. (Yes! AFTER a divorce!) Now I faithfully, with the Lord's continued help, love, support, and guidance, spread the GOOD news that nothing—NOT A THING—is impossible with God!

It is important to know that our ministry was FOUNDED to help all those who were told by pastors and Christian friends that their situations were HOPELESS. Those who come to us for hope are facing a spouse who is deep in adultery, who has moved out (often in with the other man or woman who committed adultery with), who has already filed for divorce or whose divorce has gone through. 99% of those who come, come *alone* for help since their spouse is not interested in saving their marriage, but is desperately trying to get out. Over 95% claim that they are Christians and most are married to Christians.

Over half are in some type of Christian service and many of the men who are involved with other woman are pastors who have left not only their wife and children, but their church as well.

If you, or if someone you know, is facing devastation in their marriage, there is hope. Read these awesome testimonies that prove that God is MORE than able to restore ANY marriage!

Chapter 1

Tami

"Behold, I am the LORD, the God of all flesh;
is anything too difficult for Me?"
—Jeremiah 32:27

"Delivered"

I just wanted to let God know how thankful I am for bringing me to
Restore Ministries! I have been a Christian for seven years, but before
that I was a Meth junkie and my husband was a Meth cook. I thank God
every day for delivering us from drugs, but walking out of the abuse
has been a little bit harder for me. As we all know (those He has called
He has prepared and those He has prepared He justified). We can come
to the Lord by grace and mercy or kicking and screaming. I am so in
awe at how much He loves each and every one of us!

I was a "wife of the world" who spoke her mind and had to make sure
my husband not only heard, but understood where I was coming from!
So for years after my husband and I were saved, the abuse continued
and as our child grew, she would say things that she heard my spouse
say.

Please understand, I am not trying to blame him! It was *my* own lack
of knowledge to know how to be a godly wife that fueled the fire the
enemy used against both of us! After much prayer and help from our
pastor the physical abuse, praise God, it stopped. But the verbal was so
bad I decided to get a divorce against what I knew God says and against
the advice of our pastor "A house divided against itself will not
stand"— Matthew 12:25!

It did not matter what anyone said—I was going to a divorce! I decided that the pastor did not live in my house so how could he know what was happening?! And why was God not answering me anyway?? So I leaned on what the world said.

Then one day God sent me the answer I was looking for: a new friend (Glenda) who believes God will restore her marriage! She began to explain to me about her marriage and what happened and how it took her losing her husband to finally see how to be a Godly wife and mother. She prayed with me and listened to me and then, in February 2005, she helped me to become a member and I got my books from your ministry.

Wow, it was as if a light was finally illuminating God's Word to me!!! I thought, "Could my pastor have been right?" I could now see that lots of what happened was *my* fault. But I am not saying that it is ever a woman's fault that a man is physically or verbally abusive! Because I was pushing, antagonizing and belittling my spouse, I found out I was tearing my house down with my own hands: "But the foolish tears (plucks) it down with her own hands"—Proverbs 14:1.

Soon I could see that the devil had me blinded to what I was doing wrong and only showing me what my spouse was doing wrong. You may ask yourself if I was really a *true* Christian, but God would not have shown me all this on my own.

The enemy is a liar with your money, kids, health, work, marriage, and so he attacks, destroys, and steals any good thing in your life. I was just simply blinded to everything because if he could tear my family apart, then the rest of my life would be up for grabs also.

When I married my husband I knew God brought us together and blessed us with health, finances and good children. Since becoming Christians we have stood together alone, with God. God's word says, "Two are stronger that one and three are stronger than two," also "Where there are two or three gathered together I am in the midst of it."

I just thank God for this ministry to agree with me that my marriage, my family and the peace that God gives those He loves is going to be opened to me! "Seek and you shall be given, knock and it shall be opened"—Matthew 7:7

✴ **A.S.K.** It is all right there: A=ask, S=seek, K=knock.

Words can never say how much I appreciate all this ministry has done for my family and me. I know God's hand when I feel it and I know His voice when I hear it. I'll always and forever be thankful for the day God said "Your godliness will lead you forward and the glory of the Lord will protect you from behind them." "When you call, The Lord will answer, "Yes I am here" Isaiah 58:8.

My life, my husband's life, and my children's lives will never be the same since coming here. So I say to each of you reading this, PLEASE "enter through the narrow gate, for wide is the gate and broad is the road that leads to destruction, and many enter through it but small is the gate and narrow is the road that leads to life, and only a few find it"—Matthew 7:13.

I had the opportunity to meet Erin and visit with her when she was doing her "Meeting the Members Tour" in 2005 and I was so amazed at the wisdom she had! I was just in awe!! I felt alone in my situation living with my husband and still having some of the abuse, and she just was so wise in telling me that my husband was being influenced by the enemy and I know it sounds crazy, but it gave me hope: "For he has rescued us from the one who rules in the kingdom of darkness and he has brought us into the kingdom of his dear Son"... "God has purchased our freedom with his blood and has forgiven all our sin"—Col. 1:4. And it helped me to change!!

✴ I now know that God is where my help comes from. I know to stop acting like a spoiled rotten child every time I don't get my own way: "When I was a child I used to speak like a child and think like a child, reason like a child; when I became a woman I did away with childish things"—1 Cor. 13:11. ✴

Now when things don't go the way I'd like, I know how to handle it like a Godly woman and my husband is so kind and everyone is so much happier!! Now my five children have asked, "Who are you and what have you done with our mother?" I just laugh give them a big hug and kiss and say I was here all along. I just need to find myself in God.

With all my love and prayer for all of you who believe for restoration with the same God on earth as is in Heaven.

~ *Tami in Missouri, RESTORED*

Chapter 2

Melissa

"Behold, I am the LORD, the God of all flesh;
is anything too difficult for Me?"
—Jeremiah 32:27

"A Testament"

Hi. My name is Melissa from California and this is a testament of my journey through the desert. I want to first start by thanking my Heavenly Father for how He has worked mightily in my family. It is my deepest hope that what I write here today brings great honor and glory to His Mighty name. Not a day goes by that I do not thank my Lord and Savior for every trial faced, every tear shed, every pain endured, and for every blazing inferno I had to walk through.

I have found that the Lord is my great calm, amidst the raging storm. My spiritual journey began on June 28, 2004, when my husband first made me aware of his unhappiness with our marriage and me. I couldn't have been more shocked and unprepared. You see, for the last 15 years, we truly had the all American, apple pie, white picket fence kind of life, so I thought. We never argued. I kept a neat home; we both were very involved with our children and their schools. We had a marriage and family that others viewed as flawless.

Underneath it all, much to my surprise, we had many flaws. Flaws, which I humbly admit, stemmed mostly from my own behavior. I was a very contentious, disagreeing, argumentative, irritable and anxious person. I truly edify my husband for hanging in there for as long as he did.

In July, we decided to try counseling. That was a disaster! It only lasted four sessions, with the counselor suggesting separation. My husband was in favor of taking the counselors advice. However, he was not yet prepared to leave the home. My response to my husband, "you think you can decide to leave me and then leave when it is convenient with you? I want you out by the first of the month." My first huge mistake! My husband moved on September 6, 2004. In the beginning, I did everything wrong. To the point where my husband stated, "you're going to be just like every other bitter divorcee."

This got my full attention. I refused to be a divorcee period! I fell to my knees and sought the Lord. I began applying the principles, which were embedded in me from early on. Though I had very little support or understanding from my family members, it felt right! It wasn't about allowing my husband to have his cake and eat it too. It was about honoring our blessed covenant and loving the Lord and my husband unconditionally.

In October, my dear friend in NY is who introduced to me to this ministry. I was overjoyed to have Erin confirm, what I was already putting into practice and that I was not crazy like so many tried to convince me of. At this point, it appeared we had passed through the winter season and spring was finally here. My children and I saw my husband almost on a daily basis.

He would come by most evenings after work and join us for dinner. Some nights, he would even stay over. Then the Lord decided to bless me with another cold front. In January, the Lord blessed me with another circumstance to stretch my faith. My husband was involved in adultery. Initially, I had the wind knocked out of my sails, but soon after was blessed with a peace, which surpassed all understanding.

In March, we took a family vacation during spring break. It was during this time, my husband was brought out of the darkness. He asked me to come home.

He said, "I loved you and I will spend the rest of my life making it up to you and the boys." We arrived home from vacation on March 31st and he gave his 30-day notice at his apartment on April 1st. He shut off all of his utilities and began moving his things home. One-week later, severe enemy attack began and my husband began having second thoughts.

He was experiencing manufactured feelings, which were imposed upon him by the devil and were not God's will. My husband believed he was in love with the OW. He cancelled his 30 day notice and began moving his things out again, returning to the same apartment on April 18th. Initially, I was disheartened and angry. I didn't understand why the Lord would put my children and I through this again. I fell to my knees and repented with all humility and humbleness. He reminded me that His ways are higher than our ways.

Later it was revealed to me that the Lord took my husband the second time as an answer to prayer. The first time my husband returned home, his heart was turn back to me, the wife of his youth and his children. I continued to pray that the Lord make my husband a Godly man. In order to honor my petition, I now know, it was necessary to remove my husband from the home a second time.

On April 29th, my husband left on a cross-country trip, relocating the OW to California. At this point, things changed significantly. We didn't see much of my husband, as he began working 2nd shift. He also agreed not to expose our children to the OW, as he was aware that they needed a period of healing after him leaving again. Due to his night schedule and the children not visiting his apartment, this gave him very minimal time with them.

On June 12th, our younger son invited his dad to his baptism and beach bar-b-que. The week after, he invited him to church for a Father's day special.

The following week, the message was on teenagers. My husband attended this Sunday on his own, as we have a teenager and he thought it would prove to be beneficial. Wow! Church attendance three weeks in a row! I was in complete awe at how the Lord was moving mightily in all our lives.

For the 4th of July, my two sons and I, along with my mother went away for the four-day weekend and returned late Monday night. My husband called everyday. On Tuesday morning, I got up early to take my son to school. I returned home and got back in to bed. I wasn't sleeping, but had my hand over my eyes when I heard the bedroom door open.

I assumed it is my younger son ready to start the day bright and early. Much to my surprise, it was my husband! He came in and lay down beside me. I asked him if he missed us. Then I quickly rephrased and asked if he missed the boys. He replied, "I missed the boys and I missed you." He said he was in the area, but the bank didn't open until 10:00 a.m. He wanted to know if I wanted to join him for breakfast.

Breakfast was pleasant. Initially, we just carried general conversation. Then he brought up matters, which were painful. He began sharing how he and the OW and her children had found an apartment. That they would be moving on August 1st. As always, my Heavenly Father came to the rescue. He made sure that I kept a smile on my face and maintained my gentle and quiet spirit. Inside, I was crushed. My husband has really moved on, I thought.

We left the restaurant and just when I thought things couldn't get any worse, my husband took the opportunity to continue "our talk". He said, "I've been wanting to talk with you. I was just wondering why you haven't filed any papers. It seems the next logical step. Most people in your shoes would have filed by now. I think it will add closure and help you to move on?"

Before I opened my mouth, I brought it to the Lord. I asked the Lord to give me the words. Then, I replied, "I don't know whether or not I can make you understand. Everyone has their own perspective, thoughts and opinion of things. That doesn't mean either of us is right, wrong, or indifferent. It simply means it is how we feel. I accept the fact that you have moved on. For me, a divorce decree is not a means of moving on.

I don't know what you see when you look at me, but I have moved on. This is the life that the Lord has blessed me with today and I am content. I am not too proud to admit that for me, it's either you or nobody.

I don't believe in divorce and I hope that you respect me enough to not ask me to participate. I don't need to accompany you to court. You don't even need my signature. If this is what you seek for closure, please seek it alone. I know you'll be fair to the boys and I."

Then he replied, "Here is my dilemma. I love you. I don't want to divorce you. I want to come home, but there are so many loose ends to tie up. I have been listening to this Christian radio station (I almost fell out of the truck). Last week, they talked about a father's place in the home, adultery, spiritual leadership, etc." (Was this God ordained or what!)

He proceeded to tell me that he had enjoyed going to church with us for the last 3 Sundays. He felt at peace there and that he couldn't explain it but that he definitely felt called or led by a higher source. He said that he saw things differently. I suggested, through the eyes of faith. He agreed, PTL! He turned in his 30-day apartment notice that same day.

On July 13th, my husband talked to the OW and shared with her his intentions of coming home to his family. The following morning, the adulteress was kind enough of give me a very early wake up call. She began spewing venom and the call resulted in me very quickly hanging up on her.

On Friday, July 15th, my husband moved home again. Praise God! I realize this next phase of our journey may also come with its challenges. My husband still intends to befriend the OW and her children. However, the Lord continually reminds me of Proverbs 19:21. Many are the plans in a man's heart, but it is the Lord's purpose that prevails. I am joyful in hope, patient in affliction and faithful in prayer. (Romans 12:12)

I know the Lord will remove this adulteress and her children completely from our lives, in His perfect timing. For my faith is sure of what I hope for and certain of what I do not see. (Hebrews 11:1) We serve a very faithful and honorable Lord.

I find complete comfort knowing that He leads our every step. My marriage has been restored! Our home is now built on the Rock of His Word. We no longer reside on sinking sand.

Erin, words could never begin to express how thankful I am for the unique qualities, which you possess and your willingness, which allows God to use you as a vessel to spread the Gospel.

Ladies remember, the Lord's eyes range throughout the earth to strengthen those whose hearts are fully committed to Him (2 Chronicles 16:9). Is your heart fully committed to Him? Keep looking up!

~ Melissa in California, RESTORED!

Tracie

"Behold, I am the LORD, the God of all flesh;
is anything too difficult for Me?"
—Jeremiah 32:27

"I Decided to Trust God"

If you knew my husband you would not believe that he is capable of such a sin, that is why I am writing, if it could happen to me (a person who did not have a bad marriage), it could happen to anyone who falls into sin.

My husband got reconnected (through his daughter) to his previous girlfriend in high school—old feelings and wanting "things" to be better for his daughter caused him to fall into a trap.

Yes, he had an affair (it still hurts to say it). All the books that I began reading stated God knows what we can bare and does not allow anything to happen to us that he will not receive Glory for, if we only seek Him. During this time I could not for the life of me figure out what could be HIS plan for my life.

I was so broken and I felt as if I would never be happy again. Even though I did intend to leave, I stayed because my husband assured me that it was **me** he loved and wanted our marriage to be restored.

Thankfully I knew that if I chose to leave our marriage, it would not miraculously make everything all better. I then decided to not just stay in the marriage, I decided to trust God and praise Him for my situation—even when my flesh fought against it—and, oh boy, did my flesh fight against it!

I instantly became connected with the Lord like I had never been before. In the midst of all the pain and trauma, there were some silver linings that Lord wove in. I sadly had made my husband out to be my god, he was such a good man, when it is the Lord alone who should hold that place! Men are broken vessels, and not meant to be worshiped. The searing pain of betrayal made me finally come loosed from this unhealthy dependency, and that's when He turned my heart in a fresh new way to the Living God.

God taught me forgiveness...I was very active in my church so I wondered how would I be able to teach and preach for that matter about something that I knew nothing about? That's when the Lord reminded me that HE forgave ME in a way that I will never be able to repay. That's how I forgave my husband— in a way that he will never be able to repay.

I can remember climbing in my closet because I felt so alone in the big world. I stayed there and cried out to the Lord. And I believe that God did an instant *healing* on my mind that day. It was my flesh that fought against it, not my mind or heart. If you knew me, you would say the same thing. Due to having a great deal of anxiety all of my life, I needed to be healed.

At this juncture of my life, I knew I could choose to be unhappy about this matter for the rest of my days and not represent Christ. OR I could choose to follow this Bible verse: "Brethren, I count not myself to have apprehended, but this one thing I do, forgetting those things, which are behind, and reaching forth unto those things which are before, I press toward the mark for the prize of the high calling of God in Christ Jesus."

Well, unlike most testimonies I've read recently, it was my husband who played a big role in my restoration process. He was able to walk with me while I mourned, hurt, and even was angry. It was my husband who sought God and laid the outcome at His feet. And that's how he began to "win" me all over again. He actually killed me with kindness. We began to pray together for the first time in our marriage! We give God glory each day for what HE was GOING to do even when I did not FEEL it....

~ *Tracie in West Virginia, RESTORED*

This testimony may make you feel a bit jealous until you understand that this is from a wife of one of our Encouraging Men—our Men's Marriage Restoration website. If you notice Tracie never mentioned our books because SHE didn't read them, her husband did.

The reason we are including this testimony in our Encourager and our book, is to help you SEE what is happening on the other side! Exactly what God began to do to Tracie and the role her husband played in her restoration, is how God will work on the other side.

———————Chapter 4———————

Angel

"Behold, I am the LORD, the God of all flesh;
is anything too difficult for Me?"
—Jeremiah 32:27

"Principles Leads to Restoration!!"

I believe God deserves glory and RMI deserves praise. I'm writing this because my friend doesn't *feel* completely restored. However, the details of her husband's return and how he is NOW a believer and LOVES the Word of God and seeks prayer from his wife (and me as her spiritual friend) when he feels the enemy attack are a testimony to God's power—proves she is more than RESTORED—she's blessed!!

I was personally involved from day one. It was two and a half years ago and I was Angel's neighbor. By divine appointment my crisis happened right before hers without knowing it. If fact, we first met at a neighbor's house and I shared what had happened and how I believed God for my marriage. She told me that she couldn't imagine doing the same. Well, in shock, several weeks later, she found out she had the same situation going on—her husband was living in sin and seeing an OW.

As I grew in my relationship with the Lord I shared RMI materials with her and encouraged her to become a member. For some reason she refused. She contemplated the idea but never got around to it. The thing was, she was being very real about her anger at what had happened, didn't try to hide her hurt and feelings from God.

Due to her being so real with God, He has blessed her with a restored marriage before mine! Many thought it would be me first before her because of her previously contentious ways, but God's ways are not our ways and He said the first will be last and the last will be first.

There were many false restorations, but each helped to refine Angel. She began to trust God and spend time in prayer, fasting occasionally, and crying out to her Lord and Savior. Even though she never went to the site, she was getting RMI's principles fed to her by me. I, at times, was being weighed down and so many others had abandoned her because of her insistence to do things her way instead of God's way. But God told me to hang in there with her because I was helping to save a family.

The biggest deal came when the scales were suddenly removed from her husband's eyes and he began to thirst for God's truth! It was such a blessing to see him openly share his journey and to be open about his weaknesses and ask us both for prayer. Believe me, he's the last person others thought would come to have a relationship with Jesus! He was much more blatant about being with the OW in public than my husband was (and I am thankful for that). I believe that there's a balance between not grieving God, and also not being real with Him. In other words, complicated prayers and fasting are not necessarily what God needs us to do, but it's the condition of the heart that counts.

We Christians need to recognize that being real (good or bad) is more important than ignoring the true enemies within you and drawing from your own strength. We also have to remember how individual our situations are and that God speaks to each of us according to our individual needs. That's why it's important to seek the throne and not the phone...friends will give you the right encouragement and confirm what God already has told you IF you had been spending time with Him. But if you find the wrong friend you are sunk. He wants to teach you and court you with His love and His life-giving Word. This is how you fall in love with Him. The more you lean on others the more you miss out on God's richness and deepest mysteries.

God changed this couple's situation in the twinkle of an eye when things looked absolutely hopeless—even to the point of the husband planning to move with the OW to another state to live with him—it just happened suddenly!

God's timing is not predictable, and in what way He plans to work His miracle we never know before it happens. The more we try to figure it out, the more we are off track. I discovered that it really is about our obedience, our heart condition and that God doesn't judge our outward appearance but sees the heart. As you are obedient to His Word with no exceptions, and submit to your authority (boss, parents [honor them], and husband) even when it doesn't make sense...obey!

We can't be used for His Kingdom if we think we know better. We don't know and have to instead follow Him moment by moment for His next direction. The Holy Spirit does teach, but we have to seek and in solitude will we hear! This is a journey with you and God alone...leaning on our own understanding or others will only lead to destruction and going around the mountain again and again.

God taught Angel the principles of forgiveness, prayer, fasting, faith, submission to authority, winning her husband without a word, love in action and a transparent heart (getting real with the Lord)! Now that I write this, I'm thinking this is what I've been doing. But as for Angel, I think it's because God had mercy and compassion on her and because she admits to being the person of "Oh ye of little faith." She believes God knew she and her family needed to be together.

I sometimes get concerned that Angel may have to go around the mountain again so I do pray for them. But even if she (at times) continues to do things her way, God says we must love our Christian sisters and brothers. But I do know that I have to stay close to God because God designs our path uniquely so even caution must be adhered to in every relationship; you always have to seek Him in all things and pray in all things. Never get too comfortable with an ePartner, a friend, a sister, a brother, anyone for that matter...be wise as a serpent and innocent as a dove...but always love.

God brought this couple through MANY difficult times. Oh, the difficult times were endless. The tears and pain were enormous especially seeing the kids suffer so much to witness Angel, their mom, being so weak and so filled with bitterness.

And due to this, today they have to pray so much for their children because it has made an unfavorable impact on them and caused the teenage daughter to rebel and accuse.

So though she got her marriage restored ahead of mine, I am thankful that I have not damaged my children because it would be part of the consequences that I would have to deal with later when my marriage is restored. Yes, God is faithful and is creating their father to be the spiritual leader though this!

Many times Angel took matters in her own hands, even to the point of teaching her husband what to do and not to do, AND going out of her way to talk to the OW. This only put her children and husband through a lot of pain. And also so many, many consequences she now has to deal with.

The turning point of their restoration was when God's mercy and compassion was poured on their children...I knew if it didn't happen soon, Angel would continue to take matters in her own hands and cause a more final separation and make it difficult for restoration. But God only knows for sure as I'm only an observer, and especially because Angel was much more contentious and continued to do things her way.

Even to this day we both do what we think we are led to do so I am still not sure what the turning point was. I just believe God has His ways. Still I must say that RMI is invaluable and this is what made all the difference in Angel's restoration— and mine, which is on its way!

This is how the restoration actually happened. Angel's husband came home for a spell, spent more time with the children, and then attended our church regularly (he and his family were attending another church prior to his leaving).

We just started watching how her husband began thirsting for the Word—to the point of bringing his Bible to work and praying for others! Can you believe it?!! And even when Angel began to get discourage, he would get out the Bible and read from God's Word to her to snap her out of it...it's amazing!!!

For some reason neither of them have yet put their ring back on. But I am happy to add that the OW is finally out of the picture physically (and via phone contact). But it was a long while before her husband cut all ties. He had a stronghold because the OW owed him money and he wanted her to pay, so it became a constant strain on Angel and their marriage because he needed to cut all ties.

Hallelujah, we prayed for this tie to be broken, but I know God allowed it to continue until Angel would submit to God's leading. This contact with the OW kept her on her toes. (I think we all need a thorn to keep us humble.) Our husband's hearts can turn back home instantly, but it's not until God knows that we are ready, only then, will it happen.

Ladies, we often are the reason why our husband continues to stay tied to sin. So the sooner you know God's plan and obey without delay, the sooner your husband will come back home too!!

Submitted by Jackie in California for Angel, RESTORED

Millie

"Behold, I am the LORD, the God of all flesh;
is anything too difficult for Me?"
—Jeremiah 32:27

"I'm Taking Back My Home"

Many changes have taken place in my life and I thank God that His mercy endures forever and He is a God of second, third, fourth and so on chances!!

My husband had left me for another woman back in April and is now back home!! When I first found out about the adultery my first reaction was to kick him out of my home. I don't believe it was a mistake that this happened, because in the process I came back to the Lord and found myself learning about who I am in the Lord and the strength that He has given me to live on!

The biggest breakthrough when I let my husband go! That means I **never** called him and this is what he said showed him I love him unconditionally. It proved I cared about his happiness over my own. This was very hard for me because when I loved someone I always wanted something in return.

And due to this kind of unconditional love, proving that to God and to my husband that I meant what I said about letting him go, even though he was gone for five months— he never stopped providing for his family!

He always deposited his *whole* paycheck into my account so that the bills would be paid. And in turn I made sure to tithe to this ministry from it (where I was being fed and feeding my children truths from what I learned) so that the devourer would have to leave us alone and he would have to give my husband back to us!

Thank God because it proved **He** was taking care of me. It wasn't an easy process, but I know He guided me every step of the way to know what to do by what I was learning. Even after all the good I was doing, I actually backslid right before my husband came home and began to take things into my own hands. There were areas in my life that I thought were dead, but I believe God brought them to the light so I could be rid of them before restoration would occur.

God put me through the fire to burn the impurities so that I could become a vessel of splendor, a royal diadem in His hands. I have been taking small steps by getting aligned with God and the way I began praying for the salvation of my husband. There have been severe attacks, which often make me feel like giving up on everything, but I have been able to press through due to the grace of the Almighty God. God has been given me His Word and He gave it to you too. His word is righteous and true and it's a lamp unto your feet. So be blessed and walk in that light not in the darkness like the world.

I told myself "I'm taking back my home"—Me, and my house, we ALL shall serve the Lord! This is a battlefield. The enemy doesn't just come in nicely—he comes to devour! He's tried to devour my family, my husband, my home, my children and my destiny! He's not going to be nice. I learned first about tithing to my storehouse and got fed and then the enemy had to take his hands off of us!

You have to understand this is a spiritual battle. The Lord told me that the other day that He didn't bring me this far for me to fall short of a perfect and happy live. He's showing me how to fight spiritually. He's preparing me for even greater battles that He knows are ahead of me now that my husband is home.

God brought me to the story of the Ark of the Covenant and when the glory of the Lord departed from it because they His people were disobedient. In the first battle 3,000 men died! Then in the second battle 30,000 men died. Imagine looking at a battlefield and seeing 30,000 dead bodies on the ground and all of them being men! Those men are your husbands and why you have to fight in the spirit by obeying His principles.

When men die spiritually, the women suffer, and their children suffer the most. That is why satan is after the men and using us women to get them! God commanded Adam to have dominion over the earth. Not the woman, but the man. I refuse not to believe that God cannot change any circumstance or anybody. I believe in the power of God. His Word says that nothing is too hard for Him.

His Word has to come to pass. He's not man that he should lie but it has to be in His timing and when we rush it it always takes longer. He first changes the heart of stone into the heart of flesh in the woman. He teaches her how to be obedient to Him so she will let her husband lead. It begins with respecting her husband, even if it is his decision to leave and be with another woman. By refusing we show him and God we don't respect who God put over us.

He says, "If my people would humble themselves and pray then I will heal their land." This means "I will heal their family; I will heal their children."

It's all His Word, not mine. That is the vision for your restoration. He wants each of us to speak to every mountain and every hill in our lives prophetically! Why prophetically? Because His Word shall come to pass. Not mine, but His.

~ Millie in Pennsylvania

Chapter 6

Denise

"Behold, I am the LORD, the God of all flesh;
is anything too difficult for Me?"
—Jeremiah 32:27

"Don't Ever Let Go of God's Hand!"

God is sooo awesome!! Praise Him that my marriage is restored! It is only by the grace of God that I have been given this wonderful gift, and that is exactly what it is, a gift from God. It is a gift that I am not deserving of but praise God that my Heavenly Father loves me enough to give it back to me and give me another chance to do it right!

I had been separated from my husband for 4 years. We had only been married 4 years when I was the one who told my husband I didn't love him anymore and I moved out.

When I think about it, my heart aches at the pain I caused him. He is a wonderful man and husband but I thought I wanted something more, the "fairy tale" love. When you watch TV and read books and see how "perfect" everything seems, you start to think that that is reality when it's not.

Finally, after 3 years, God led me to stop and think about the important things in life. He showed me all the gifts He had already given me and how I had squandered them. I thought about how much time (and money) I had wasted on all this nonsense. He then began to turn my heart back toward my husband.

But even in the midst of all of this realization, I was still the same person I was before, argumentative, stubborn and opinionated. One day, after a particularly bad day at work, I had an argument with my husband on the phone and I finally said to him, "Either put forth an effort on our relationship or divorce me!" I can't even believe I said those words. Who was I to say those things when I hadn't even changed?

It was only 1½ months after I said those words that he took me up on my offer and told me he wanted a divorce. I was in shock. I never thought he would divorce me. Somewhere in the back of my mind I always thought we would get back together because it was the "right" thing to do, not necessarily because it was a "good" thing to do.

Needless to say, I was devastated. I got to the point where I could barely function. I couldn't eat and either I couldn't sleep or I slept all the time. I cried constantly. Everyone who knew me used to joke that I didn't have a heart because I never showed emotion. After that, I couldn't hide my emotions. People at my work never even knew I was separated. I had kept it a secret until that point because I was embarrassed.

I had finally reached my breaking point. I had been a Christian since I was a teenager but I never really had a relationship with the Lord. I knew that I had nowhere left to turn except to God. I decided to switch churches back to the one I grew up in. I knew they loved and served the Lord with all their hearts. I started going to church more and praying.

It was still difficult. I was still emotional and didn't know what to do. My husband and I still had some contact but it was so hard every time to say good-bye. Finally, about 1½ months later, I felt like we had a huge breakthrough, but after the holidays he went back to thinking we should get divorced.

Then I finally found the RMI website after searching for prayer sites on line. I had prayer requests in everywhere I could find but it wasn't until I ordered their materials (right away) and started reading the "Restore" book that I immediately started following its instructions.

I also started praying more, reading my Bible, and fasting. I started listening to praise music at work and while driving in the car. God gave me such a peace; I couldn't believe it.

Whatever His will was for me, I was going to be happy!

I had always believed in prayer, but never really spent much time in it. It was amazing that when I started praying for things, big or small, my prayers would get answered. I had been a Christian for so long, why should this amaze me so much?

My husband finally sought individual counseling from a counselor. I figured this would surely be the end knowing what I had learned about the destruction of counseling. At his first session his counselor told him he should step back from me! It seemed we would never recover from what his counselor told him to do. But I wouldn't give up and stop believing. I did what the Lord asked and kept praying.

My husband noticed all the changes in me but thought they were just temporary. He thought I was doing whatever I could so he wouldn't divorce me. One evening he said to me that he told his counselor he didn't know why he was wavering in his decision for a divorce. He said usually when he makes a decision, he sticks with it. But I knew why, it was the Lord!

Eventually we started spending more time together. Finally, he asked me to join him on vacation with some of his family members. While on vacation, we talked about our relationship and he told me I could move home at any time and that he did in fact love me!!

As soon as we got home I went and got my clothes packed and I haven't left since!!

God is so amazing! Our new relationship is wonderful! God has taught me so much over the past year: patience, humility, and steadfastness. I love my new relationship with the Lord even more.

I used to think that I shouldn't "bother" God with trivial things, there are so many more important problems in the world, but then I always remember that if He loves us enough to number the hairs on our heads, then He cares about EVERYTHING in our lives!

My husband is not yet saved but I know that God will save him! I know I blew my witness to him and many others by my actions over the years and that also makes my heart ache, but this time will be different!

I now pray that God uses me as a witness to lead souls to Him!

I apologize that this is so long but I prayed about this for a while because I wanted to say what God wanted me to. I wanted to be able to give God the glory and also encourage others.

Don't ever let go of God's hand!!!

~ Denise in New York, RESTORED

Chapter 7

Ginger

"Behold, I am the LORD, the God of all flesh;
is anything too difficult for Me?"
—Jeremiah 32:27

"It Came & Went"

Looking back, I never really had a personal relationship with God. I thought I did (just like everyone else thinks they do) because I attended church regularly and prayed. But the actions and words were just being done mechanically. Then when my husband and I started dating, even this went by the wayside. It was the beginning of the end.

Our relationship was rocky right from the start and only got worse as time went on. I know now that I had some emotional issues that hadn't been dealt with and he had some trust issues and other feelings left from being in the Vietnam War. He also drank a lot. Things only got worse— to the point where I started becoming violent, throwing things, and pushing and hitting him.

Despite knowing and experiencing all of this, we married anyway. There were no issues of infidelity on either part, just a huge lack of respect and unconditional love. There was always tension between us and we fought about stupid things all the time.

The violence on my part continued. I even called the cops twice and threatened him with a gun. He tried in his own way to help me by taking me to doctors to try to get some help, and they ended up giving me a lot of medication. It didn't do any good!

After a major blowout one day, my husband had had enough and left. We were both angry and told everyone we were getting divorced. We even went to a divorce mediator. After about a month I felt really horrible and tried to talk to my husband. He was cold and simply uncaring. However, three months later I managed to persuade him to come back home. I still hadn't formed a relationship with the Lord at this point, but He was right there with me, giving me another chance. Things were okay for a while, but without Him in my life, of course things went back to the way they were very quickly.

My husband left again about 6 months later. And once again, we told everyone that it was over. We even put our house up for sale. Then it happened. One morning I got up early and went to an exercise club for women near my house. My husband had begged me to join some type of exercise program for months, but I wouldn't. It was at this exercise place that I met a wonderful woman who I know God sent to me. She stuck up a conversation with me and I found myself telling her my situation. She gave me a book to read, and as you might have guessed, it was your book.

Slowly but surely things began to come together once I was given the truth. I finally realized how badly I had treated my husband and how it was because I had been living without God in my life. This woman became a good friend, as she helped me get through some tough days by pointing me back to God, to His Word and to your book.

I decided to look online for Restore Ministries website. After stumbling through other books and websites claiming to know the secret of restoring marriages I found you. It was so clear that they weren't the real deal promising all sorts of things based on things that were not backed up by His Word.

The entire Restore Ministries website was nothing but encouraging! It talked mostly about the Lord, about His Word, and quoted verses upon verses from the Bible. I ordered all of Erin's books and poured over them night after night after night. And then, I finally got it!

I realized I lost sight of God and all His goodness. I had become a contentious woman.

I cried and cried when I realized what had happened. I asked for God's forgiveness and repented. I forgave myself, my husband, and others from things I'd done or what had been done to me in the past.

Immediately, I began to feel better even though my situation looked very bleak. Little by little I saw the changes that He was doing in me. Immediately I began to lose the 30 pounds I had gained since I got married. My prayer life meant so much to me now, more than anything else in my life. I began to learn how to talk to God and to understand His Word!

My husband however was adamant about the divorce. He even said he was moving to another state. He said he had no feelings for me any more. We got a court date for the divorce, and with the help and encouragement of my ePartner (Yes, the woman who first gave me my book was hanging out there for women like me) I was able to make it through.

My ePartner reminded me not to look at what circumstances that were surrounding me, but instead to focus on what mattered. So I worked feverishly on my relationship with the Lord above all else. God worked so quickly in me as I continued to put my trust in Him. I realized that the Lord was my Husband and that my relationship with Him was the most important of all. I spent hours all night praying and communing with the Lord.

Then I watched in amazement how God began to soften my husband's heart. And He also had arranged things so that we were okay financially during this time.

Once I began to tithe from both our incomes, even though my husband never knew, never asked, and only said to make sure I paid all the bills, which I did. My first commitment was to the Lord because I knew how else would the enemy be rebuked? Soon after I got brave enough to tithe on my husband's paycheck, my husband got a new full time job after working sporadically for years!

Once he got a job he felt better, he would call and we began to speak on the telephone a little. Once in a while I would run into him somewhere around town. Things were awkward at first, but we began to have good conversations always initiated by him.

Everyday I practiced the principles in Erin's books, which taught me how to keep things in perspective, and, boy they really worked! As long as I kept my eyes on the Lord, my heart turned towards Him, was faithful in my tithing and obedient to what I knew God wanted me to do, my husband and I began seeing each other a little more. Each time he would see me or talk to me, my husband said he was noticing so many changes in me.

God guided me all the way—He is so good! My husband and I really started to like each other again, and believe it or not, the court date came and went!!

Before all this happened in my life, I never even owned a Bible! So I bought the one geared for children and could not believe what it contained. Everything I needed to know was right there in black and white. The passages from Scripture in Erin's books smacked me right in the face each time I would read through it. Boy, I needed that! For years I hit my husband, now God was hitting me with His Word, but it felt so good. I now know the order of things in marriage, in family, and most importantly what order the Lord and God needs to be in a person's life. I realize for the first time, as a wife, that I should be in submission to my husband as unto the Lord (meaning I am doing it because of my love for Him). I also learned that I need to be tolerant and patient not only with my husband — but with everyone!!

I learned that my purpose here on earth is to love everyone by how my ePartner loved me, even before she knew me. She wasn't exercising to get her body fit, but was there looking for others to help, women like me (and so many other women who are now part of our fellowship that meets at her house).

Before this I had always worried about everything, focusing only on me. Now since I began looking and finding other women to help, I no longer worry about anything! It was when I began giving my troubles up to God for the first time in my life that I had a peaceful feeling inside! No more medication and no more focusing on me!

After being separated for four months, my husband came back home!!! I give thanks and praise to God! Our relationship is better than it has ever been all because my relationship stays strong and focused on my true Husband, the Lord. My husband has not found Christ yet, but he knows that I have Him and has seen all the positive things that have come out of it.

My husband continues to have me tithe from his paycheck, which has kept our finances good and at an all-time high. He also encourages me to read my Bible while he reads his. He's spoken about taking me to church, but I am still waiting. I am trusting God to bring Him through a similar experience like He took me through. And in the meantime, I have my Husband with me and I know I am His bride now, not just the special one He'll come back for.

I know life is full of ups and downs, but I know that I will get through them with God right by my side. I will never, ever lose sight of Him again!!

For all you women praying and believing God for restoration, remember, "With God all things are possible." Once He becomes your "everything" then everything will be given to you.

~ Ginger in Rhode Island

Chapter 8

Lee Ann

"Behold, I am the LORD, the God of all flesh;
is anything too difficult for Me?"
—Jeremiah 32:27

"Jeremiah's Lesson"

I met my husband 12 years ago. I had two children, and he had two children, and without even marrying, we moved in together. I was very uneasy about this, as I knew God well enough to know that He would not bless us. Things were great for only a year until he suddenly moved out! He was a musician and we were each very immature and self absorbed!

We reconciled a few months later and then married. After a year, he left again! We reconciled 3 years later after we began dating for a while. Four months later, he left and filed for divorce, which was final 3 months later. I went to God every time between his walkouts, but didn't stay in His Word. When things were fine, I simply felt I didn't need God. However, I started keeping a prayer journal and I asked God to take away my desire for my husband or else send him back to me.

I didn't hear anything from him for a very long time, so I felt that God would send someone else to me. As it turned out, once I made the Lord my Husband, He sent my husband back to me when I didn't even want to be married ever again, not to my ex or anyone else!

My ex-husband began writing and singing Christian music and attending church, so this is what first got my attention, but I was still not interested in giving up what I had with the Lord as my Husband.

Two years later, however, I gave into God's will and we remarried, and immediately bought a house. I assured God that I would stay in His word this time! But it is much harder to remain faithful to the Lord when there is a husband in the home, which is why I begged God not to have my husband pursue me (and why I didn't want to remarry him).

As soon as I lost sight of the Lord, when He wasn't first as He had been, that was when my husband's 18 yr. old daughter took over. I watched myself become very contentious and mouthy about him spending thousands of dollars on her, rescuing her from her consequences. He had let her mistreat me and did not defend me, but scolded me instead. I heard God's voice telling me to watch it, but I didn't care!

Just as the verse says, that is who I became. Proverbs 5:4, "But in the end she is bitter as wormwood, Sharp as a two-edged sword."

My husband left after 3 years, and moved in with his daughter in an apartment that he co-signed for her to get against my wishes. Just as Proverbs 21:9 "It is better to live in a corner of a roof than in a house shared with a contentious woman."

His daughter is whom I dealt with instead of an OW, which I guess is not as bad as so many of you so I have no reason to complain. My husband was very angry with me, and was very concerned about his daughter who had no respect for him either and showed it. I felt that I took better care of him, and yet he left me to go live with her! How much proof does anyone need to see that this is a spiritual battle, nothing that can be won in the flesh?

I, of course, cried out to God in my hurt and rejection. During this same time, my mother passed away so that is what further broke me.

My husband seemed very unconcerned, and of course, I was devastated! I began to absorb the Bible more and more, and at my Mother's funeral I decided to begin rereading the Restore Your Marriage book. I read it constantly, it was so comforting when I began thinking of restoring my marriage to my Beloved Husband, Jesus! I think that I read all the testimonies on the website 5 times trying to absorb the true concept of whose I was supposed to be restored to!!

This time, I believed for my marriage restoration to my true Husband. About the same time my husband said he found a "Christian" counselor and as said, "she could tell you that you are in the wrong." In obedience I did go, but she didn't say that.   Yet, as you warn in your books regarding counseling and counselors, true to your warning this "Christian" counselor was sure to emphasize each time that we needed to stay separated. We saw her a total of 5 times and were even farther away from restoration! What was worse is that all of it made my husband numb towards God and angry towards me. Thank God I didn't go with any hope or expectations like I once had (before coming here to your ministry), like everyone else who believes counseling will help when it is the most destructive thing you can do to a marriage.

Sometimes, my husband said we should "talk" and due to what he did in counseling, he would name all my failures and be ever so unforgiving the more he spoke about them. Each time I was confessing them, but then one day I reread in your book that it would be better if I kept silent. The phrases: **"Won without a word"** and "wait on the Lord" began running through my mind. Then he found a Christian couple that "counseled" in their home who had been married 56 years.

Instead of talking about our problems, they had us read Bible verses about anger, marriage, and forgiveness. They did not give us a chance to argue and tell each other's wrongs. They talked about what God desires, and that it is impossible to have a solid marriage without Jesus!

 In between these appointments, my husband wanted to get the house ready to sell and we had a realtor.

We hadn't signed any papers yet, but he was talking as if he wasn't sure we would live together ever again. This was fine with me because I had the Lord and I could see that bothered my husband because he couldn't figure it out.

I worried and fretted that God would ask me to allow restoration again, and that is when, I had to get a hold of God, and be still. The last few days I cried out to God and was sobbing because I just wanted Him. I cried "How many times are you going to let me go through these separations and reconciliations with this man? How much am I supposed to take? How can you ask this of me?"

I can't remember a time I was so broken! But the darkest is always before the joy in the morning! That same night my husband called me, and said he didn't want to sell the house! He said a peace came over him, and the Holy Spirit had shaken him. He said "I'll be home this weekend Babe, if you want me back."

What could I say? I had studied the verse in 1 Corinthians 7:13 "And a woman who has an unbelieving husband, and he **consents** to live with her, she must **not send** her husband away." But what about the other verse, Proverbs 5:4, "But in the end she is bitter as wormwood, sharp as a two-edged sword." What would keep me from becoming like that woman again? That verse speaks about an adulteress, and as long as I am faithful to my true Husband, then I am no adulteress— I am His beloved Bride!!

For everyone who is reading my testimony, restoration does happen quick and unexpected! That is why you need to make sure you are ready! While I was so grief stricken and searching God's word, He kept taking me to the book of Jeremiah. I felt like He was telling me not to keep turning away from Him after He delivers me out of my trouble or He would bring me through the same lessons over and over again — until I learned it! Now I will hold fast to my Lord and Master, and love my Husband, even in the good times with my earthly one!!

Thank you Erin for your encouragement and comfort! You have truly been a faithful servant!

~ Lee Ann in Tennessee

Chapter 9

Chelle

"Behold, I am the LORD, the God of all flesh;
is anything too difficult for Me?"
—Jeremiah 32:27

"My Husband Called Me Beautiful"

It began Christmas Eve, 2000, when my husband took me out to dinner. I remember that trip through the country roads that night dotted with Christmas lights and wishing the children could see them. For many years after this, the mere sight of Christmas lights made me want to throw up.

My husband told me he had something to show me before we ate and drove through a neighborhood then stopped in front of a house. My heart took a flip—I thought he was going to show me "our" new house that we had been hoping for. Instead, he turned to me and said, "We have had 20 wonderful years together, but . . ." So I laughed and said, "Are you dumping me?" He continued to tell me that there was no one else but that he no longer loved me (I had killed all love), and he wanted to "be in love again"!

This house was where he was moving to—it was one hour from me and the children. He said he knew I had my heart's desire with all the children (we had six), and I would be just fine.

I walked right into that house and fell into a ball in the bathroom and was very sick. Some how I made it out of the bathroom and asked him if it would make a difference if we put some of the children up for adoption.

I cringe at that memory still—but I know God has forgiven me. Somehow we made it through dinner, and I asked him if it could possibly be with me that he could "fall in love again"? He was being flip, but he said, "With God all things are possible!" God had given me hope in the words of my husband!

That night, the devil reminded me that years ago my husband had said that when I turned 40, he would trade me in for two 20-year-olds. This was more true than I knew. He had been working nights and was out of town very often. It was not unusual for the children to not see him for weeks at a time. He moved during the night, and I offered him everything he needed. The children were all very young and were used to me giving things away or letting friends borrow furniture—so they did not notice that he was gone. I don't remember much of the next six weeks. I remember lots of alcohol and prescription drugs. I must have purchased at least 40 books from the Christian bookstore on marriage and divorce. I wanted to keep the children innocent, and I was so ashamed. I told very few people what had happened.

I had no desire to seek revenge—I simply wanted my husband to love me again. I took a good look at myself in the flesh. I was bald (from chemo), took no care in my appearance, I drank too much, I was extremely overweight, and I was in the middle of reconstruction surgery for cancer. I can only imagine what my friends would think of my husband if they knew he had left me and abandoned the children.

Then I took a deeper look, and saw what the world and my friends did NOT know—that I had not allowed my husband to be intimate with me for over a year.

I never went with him when he invited me out for fun (my children needed me), and I de-edified him in front of my children. I had become everything I later learned God did NOT want a wife to be. I was contentious, proud, a huge liar, an arrogant Pharisee, and so much more. No wonder he left me—I was a FOOL! I wrote him a letter telling him all of these things—which I do NOT recommend at all, as it only reinforced the "hate wall." (It was not until months later when I was able to tell him these things to his face that he truly saw I had changed.)

About six weeks after he left, he called to confess that he had indeed fallen in love with someone (many months before), but she could not leave her husband as my husband had hoped, and she had broken his heart. I never knew who this person was until the week my husband decided to come home. Believe me—I tried to find out.

I remember a night going through two 55-gallon garbage cans looking for credit card receipts, but God protected me using my own husband— He had taken the receipts with him that night after he said goodnight to the children! Years later, he told me that she had loved me too much to destroy our family.

During this time, I think I had lost over 30 pounds with the "infidelity diet" (later, with proper exercise, prayer, and fasting, I lost a total of 85 pounds). I had purchased a few new clothes and a wig. I also found, in one of those books I had purchased, that I could actually receive counseling from the author on the phone for $150 an hour. I deceived my husband into joining me in a session to "help me" and he agreed. When it was my husband's turn in the session to talk in private, of course I put my ear to the door and heard things that my heart was never meant to hear.

Several thousand dollars later, I realized this "expert" had not gone through what I was going through—so how could he possibly lead me? I went onto his chat line in search of help and saw a reference to RMI in a note to someone else.

I went back the next night hoping it was still there and logged on to RMI right away. Praise God! I am sorry to say that I did not read anything on the web that night—but, I went right to the order department and saw something called "Suggested Package." I didn't know who had suggested it, but I needed something! Praise God for His hand on my life!!

When I received the materials, I read the How God Can and Will Restore Your Marriage book—and conviction came upon me. I prayed for God to change me and apologized to those people who listened to me shame my husband.

My pastor and I agreed to disagree on the subject of restoration principles. Now he gets the biggest smile on his face when we visit our old "home church" and my husband can sit in the front row without shame, because his wife found the Truth in God's Word through RMI!

When I listened to the "Be Encouraged" videos, I found hope. When I read A Wise Woman book, I had a road map written to help me through God's Word for my very own restoration!

One day, a special package came from an attorney's office, and I was in a fleshly panic. I brought the mail to where my husband was working (which he did ask me to do that day), and all I could think of was "My grace is sufficient!" I repeated it all the way to his workplace. My husband quickly dismissed it as relating to work, and I smiled and breathed a huge sigh of relief and silent praise to God. (I, of course, feared that they were divorce papers.)

That day when I got home, I started to make 3x5 cards with Scripture that was special to me. If you have read A Wise Woman, you know that RMI encourages us to do this. I started to read the book, but I had ignored that specific instruction. Now I knew why we need those little "swords of the spirit"! I still have my original stack of cards, and I am using them right now as I write this testimony. Some of them are folded and worn from when I used to carry them in my back pocket.

My first prayers for restoration were from these cards of Scripture. I would simply say, "Dear Lord—Scripture verse—in Jesus' name, amen." As I prayed these simple prayers, I saw the "hate wall" crumble!

"And Jesus said unto them, 'Because of your unbelief: for verily I say unto you, if ye have faith as a grain of mustard seed, ye shall **say** unto this mountain, remove hence to yonder place; and it shall remove; and nothing shall be impossible unto you'" (Matt. 17:20 KJV).

My next leap into prayer came in the form of song. I would play praise and worship music whenever I could and sing by myself or with the children. The words of my own restoration songs are still hidden in my heart today. I noticed that as my songs of joy increased, so did the visits from my husband! When he would visit, I would leave him alone with the children—and he would follow me around the house!

With my faithful stack of 3x5 cards, I started to minister to others in need. As I began to pray for others, my husband began to ask me out on dates.

Then I started my prayer journal with a page for myself, my husband, the other woman (women), and each of my children. As often as I could, when the children had gone to bed, I would fervently pray the prayers from each page. This meant no TV, a real biggie for me!

Soon my little prayer journal became a praise journal as well. I was able to cross off many of these prayers on a daily basis. I would hear my husband say things exactly word for word as I had prayed them. Praise God! Sometimes, I had to turn my head from giggling at God's mercy and goodness to me.

I would love to say that the moment that RMI came into my life, my husband came home and we lived happily ever after—but that was not the case. I did continue to become more attractive to my husband on the outside, and my husband was noticing a change on the inside as well. He was not, however, quite sure it was for real—and quite frankly, neither did I.

I soon fell into the pit of being the "husband pleaser" instead of walking the road of "submitting to him as unto the Lord." Big mistake!! One night, on a date, he took me to a new place, and I innocently followed him in as he had asked me to. It was a strip club.

I sat down, and he started to explain that this is where he had been spending his free time (and lots of money), because he could be "loved" without the complications of being involved. (He has given me permission to share this story and does know that he was deep in sin and battling demons at this point in his life.)

I immediately began to pray as we sat down and very quickly all the women began to come up to me and praise my husband. They said he "was a gentleman" and always took the time to listen to their problems. I was comforted and sickened at the same time. When one of the girls had heard that I was a cancer survivor, she took me back to the dressing room and young girl after young girl began to come to me for prayer. I don't think I was very good for business that night.

I would like to say that I never went back to that place, but as I said, I fell into the husband- pleasing pit, and I willfully followed him back many times.

God had provided a way out, because my husband would always ask if I minded going, but I never said no. Of that I am ashamed and have long since been forgiven.

I noticed that when I would spend the night at my husband's house after a date, our intimacy would be missing "love" and I felt "used," much as I am sure those girls felt each night they went to work. I continued to praise God that I was blessed with time alone with my husband and with intimacy no matter the circumstances.

I knew I needed to take one more step in my prayer life, and with the encouragement of the words on the videos, I did. I asked for and received the baptism of the Holy Spirit.

Now I was fully equipped and filled with the boldness only the Holy Spirit can provide. At that moment, I "knew" that my husband would come home and whatever happened before that was not the "Truth."

When my husband would say he was coming home (which happened several times) and then several weeks later want to have a "talk" with me, I could listen to his words of rejection with a gentle and quiet spirit and pray in my spirit silently. In fact, I found that I was able to stay in prayer all day. I found myself walking around the house just talking with my best friend, Jesus.

The more time I spent talking with Jesus, the more time my husband chose to spend at home, until he came home for good. I was covered with the blood of Jesus, and I knew I had the power to overcome all evil!!

"I have given you authority to trample on snakes and scorpions and to overcome all the power of the enemy; nothing will harm you" (Luke 10:19 NIV).

Then in January of 2002, my husband spent a week at home. We had enjoyed a wonderful Christmas week with the children and his family (who did not know the circumstances).

I woke up one morning at four in the morning, and I saw my husband with his gym bag (this was not unusual for him to get up and go work out) so I kissed him good-bye, and he said he was going to spend a few days back at his house, and he would call me later.

The next day, a friend pulled up in his truck, and I went outside to tell him my husband was not home. He told me that his wife and my husband had gone away together and began to say things about my husband that I did not want to hear. I quickly told him to go home and wait for his wife to come home and discuss these things with her. Praise God he left quickly, and the children never knew he was there.

My husband called that night and said, "I heard you had some excitement today at the house." I told him that it was "no more than usual," not alluding to the magnitude of the "visit."

He told me he would be back in town the next day, and he would be staying at his house. He showed up the next night on his way to work. I remained quiet while he said he could no longer afford two homes and would be moving back soon. He had said this before (so this time I did not jump up and down) but simply smiled and asked him if he wanted us to bring him dinner at work.

He came home in the morning after his shift and received a phone call when I was in the shower. It was his brother, and he was describing the weekend with the OW and so much more that I did not want to hear. I didn't know what to do, so I just left the bathroom as soon as I could and he knew I had heard. He slept that day in our bed, and when I came in to wake him for his next shift, he held me gently and told me he had no idea why he had gone away with her after not seeing her for over a year—but that I was the one he wanted to be with. Praise God!

In February, he came home, and in April, he put his wedding band back on—but I still did not have his heart. I walked on eggshells for many months. The devil tried to convince me that he would not stay. He was laid off from his job; we lost our home, a car, and fell into a financial ruin bigger than I have ever seen (and I was CPA for many years).

God is still working on me, but my greatest joy comes in answered prayers that I put in my precious prayer journal on those nights years ago when Jesus was my only Husband.

God is completing our restoration. It has been three years since my husband put back on his wedding ring, and for the past few months, I have been the poster child for how NOT to be a wise woman. I know my flesh is struggling as my husband is taking over his rightful place as the head of our home and becoming the spiritual leader. I had these roles for so long that it is very uncomfortable to give them up.

Now God is using my own husband to draw me closer to Him. (God is so funny.) The more contentious I become, the more my husband hugs me and says he has never loved me so much, and he appreciates everything I do. I praise God for answered prayer.

The more of a Pharisee I become, the more my husband quotes Scripture to me or sings of his love for God. He raises his arms without shame in church, and my children follow his example. He insists the children come to "big church" with us. I praise God for more answered prayer.

The spirit of depression was on me the other morning, and my husband came in and sang to me, "God is the strength of my heart!" I cried for this answered prayer.

When I was angry and frightened that his salary was cut yet again, my husband said, "God promised us our 'daily bread'—He will not leave us!" Praise Him again for answered prayer.

When the children misbehave, my husband started to discipline them—but very firmly. I am learning to trust God and praise Him for this too.

When I was having a pity-party about my extreme weight gain, my husband said, "We need to start 'date night' again," and we were blessed with a restaurant gift certificate. That night my husband called me beautiful. God is so full of grace. I will continue to praise Him as long as I have breath.

I never really had a true 'ePartner,' but I do have a special friend who continues to remind me that I deserve nothing God has ever given me (including my husband and my restoration)—but that through His grace alone He has and will continue to bless me!!

I will not throw my gift of restoration away—I am going to fight the good fight of faith and allow Him to continue to mold me into the wife and mother He means for me to be. I am His child, and He is no respector of persons. What he did for me—He is more than able to do for you!

~ *Chelle in Alabama*, RMI Fellowship Member, RESTORED!!

Chapter 10

Kimberly

"Behold, I am the LORD, the God of all flesh;
is anything too difficult for Me?"
—Jeremiah 32:27

"Home to Stay"

In October of 2003 my husband came to me one day and said he wasn't happy in our marriage — he told me that he was going to leave. He left and during this time we only talked if it concerned bills or something of importance.

Then one day he came and admitted he had been in adultery and now there was a child. I was devastated because we had tried to have children and it hadn't happened yet. I didn't think I would be able to go on with my life! I didn't know which way to turn. I was down and depressed and suicidal. When I went home for the holidays, my cousin took me to speak to a pastor friend of hers who was affiliated with this ministry.

As she talked and told me "all things were possible with GOD" and we could ask "anything in HIS name and HE will do it," my eyes began to open to GOD!

I began to read Scriptures and the Bible on a daily basis. I read and reread your book on marriage, which was based solely on GOD'S Word. Then after the New Year, GOD lead me to the Restore Ministries' website, which led me to your Encouraging Women website. Wow what a day!!

The additional resources you offered, all for free, helped me so much because they opened my eyes and showed me even more that "all things were possible with GOD"! I now knew the more of the truth! They showed me that GOD loves marriages and wants to heal and restore marriages but for the right reason, not for the reason the world gives us.

Every book and lesson you offered, again for free, was each was so helpful! I was given an ePartner and this was very helpful as long as we stayed focused and encouraged each other to keep pursuing the Lord. Daily we shared words of encouragement from the Bible, sending each other verses that began with marriage, then our marriage to the Lord as His bride, then more and more of His love for us that everything else faded away. I could always count on my ePartner to help lift me up when I began to fall for my husband, which is easy to do when he begins coming around and being kind again.

It helped having someone that understands the things you're going through and how you are feeling. But I admire your ministry so much for not giving me my ePartner until I was ready or I would have turned to her and also we would have talked about our estranged husbands, not the Lord and on our marriage restoration, rather than what He is calling us to do and why we went through this (to help others).

I began praying for my relationship with GOD soon after coming here. That moved to praying for myself to have the relationship with the Lord and no longer be a spiritual adulteress to Him. I stopped praying for my husband (because it made me long for him and not the Lord), and stopped praying for our marriage too — believing that it was possible for me to have a restored marriage as soon as my spiritual marriage to Him was right.

Slowly I began to read HIS Word and look to HIM for guidance, for love, for support, for comfort and for companionship, and He helped me to see my own sins and things that I did that were wrong in order for me to confess them (to Him then my ePartner) and once I repented I began to feel lighter and freer and cleaner.

At one point, I knew I needed to ask for my husband for forgiveness but not until GOD showed me how to have a gentle and quiet spirit and not get heart entangled with him. HE helped me to become stronger in Him and look to HIM each time I faced something difficult and anytime I was hurting. I learned to come to HIM with all my concerns and depend on HIM and most of all to trust HIM. I learned to agree with my husband even when I didn't want to because of what I was agreeing to. And I learned to submit to my husband and support him because my first commitment was to the Lord who asks us to do it.

As I began trusting and believing GOD, my husband began calling me more and coming over to see me. Then it got to the point where he would come over to stay. He still wouldn't say whether he wanted us to be together or not, but I kept on believing and trusting GOD because I no longer wanted it. Then it got ridiculous to the point where he was calling 3-4 times a day and staying over at least 2-3 times a week making my time with the Lord shorter and shorter.

Whenever he needed something he would call me for help and now I was able to see how things were turned around. It was like he always wanted me around and would find an excuse for me to be around. This happened the more I kept trying to get rid of him and spending time with him, so I could be alone with the Lord. It is just like Erin says. I know she experienced it too, but I am still amazed how right she was.

As I said, I had learned to have gentle and quiet sprit and how to submit to my husband even when I didn't want to, but to trust GOD. I learned how to stand in faith and believe GOD no matter what was said and done during this time all because I wanted to be obedient to Him.

I no longer wanted my marriage restored and just as Erin said, that is when my husband wanted it. Though this time of my husband pursing me because I was pursing the Lord, I learned to depend on GOD through it all no matter the situation and to thank and praise HIM for the good and the bad.

I learned to let my husband be the head and I was to be his helpmate, not the other way around. This was easy when I became the Lord's bride because I took all my needs to Him.

I learned never to return evil for evil but return evil with good.. something I would ask the Lord to tell me what I was to give in return. This wasn't just in my marriage but in all my relationships.

There were times when people were telling me my husband was with someone else, even my own family would tell me this. But I no longer cared because restoration was no longer my goal. Sometimes I would be so down and out that all I could do was call on the name Jesus and it got me through. I was concerned about what God would do about this innocent child and wanted so much to tell my husband to just marry this other woman so his child would have a home, but I knew I needed to trust God for His plan and not make my plan happen.

During those difficult nights when my mind would be in a whirl, focusing on the Lord got me to sleep. Especially through holidays or special occasions when my husband would want to spend them with me, but I thought he should spend them with his child. But no matter what, HE was there for me and brought me through as I prayed His will be done.

About 3 weeks after a really tough week, his sister found out she had to move, which meant my husband did too because he lived with her. So he was in search of his own apartment and I became nervous he would ask to move home. When he asked me to help him search, I didn't like the idea, but I did it anyways and continued to pray because I didn't trust myself to be impartial.

My spiritual encourager began to tell me to hold on and believe even more because GOD can and will turn situations around when you least expect it and turn it the right way!

That's when my husband asked me if he gave me the money would I go pay his deposit because they were going to move on Friday to live with the other woman and his child. So I did that on Thursday for him. And it was during these 2 weeks of him moving, I began to feel anxious and felt really bad about him moving to a new place and that this is the way I had been praying for things to turn out. So I began to trust and ask GOD for HIS will and not giving me the desires of my heart, but His plan.

It was way out of town that I drove to pay his deposit, and one day when I was in this town again, he called me and asked me to drive by and get his deposit back because he thought of something else and would it be alright if we could discuss it later! So I did and I knew not to ask him what he intended to do.

That evening he came by and we went to get the car washed and he looked at me and said he was coming home to his wife and make things work because I was the wife of his youth and that he truly loved me and not the other woman.

He repented for leaving and said he didn't know how to stay with me and face me knowing what he had done by fathering a child. And that he knew he needed time, living with his sister to know what God wanted him to do. That he knew he was supposed to be home and in time have me help him make a home for his child. Though this is not the way I thought I would become a mother, God's ways are much higher than His ways!!

Without saying anything unkind about the other woman, I know this is God's best and I am going to do all I can to help her become a good mother to this special child too.

I know I will need to be careful to not hurt or harm anyone, but again "all things were possible with GOD" and when I ask "anything in HIS name and HE will do it," so that my eyes again will to open to GOD and His plan!

LORD I JUST WANT TO THANK YOU — YOU WERE THERE FOR ME EVEN WHEN I DIDN'T DESERVE IT. YOU ARE FAITHFUL TO YOUR WORD AND ALL YOU ASK IS TO DO THE SAME!!

~ *Kimberly in North Carolina*, RESTORED and a soon-to-be mother to my husband's child!

Chapter 11

Joan

"Behold, I am the LORD, the God of all flesh;
is anything too difficult for Me?"
—Jeremiah 32:27

"All the Answers"

After 23 years of marriage, which included 12 years of ministry throughout the United States and Canada, my husband left our home on October 1 and the divorce was final eight months later in June.

Seven years does seem like a long time, but God has changed us both in many, many ways for His kingdom, and for our personal growth. Nonetheless, He has never failed either one of us, nor our three children. Our youngest was 12 when her father left, and she is now 19. So the years do pass, and thankfully the healing is all in God's hands, and most amazingly, it takes only a moment, an instant, when He changes it all—as He always does—suddenly!!

It was a Sunday when my husband came over and we were just talking about "stuff" and then he somehow steered the conversation around to asking me to marry him! Wow, what a surprise. I had long given up and moved on with my life. When it finally happened, it was gentle and very pleasant! Even though my children knew about it, and I believed that God would restore our marriage someday when I first began this journey, it came as a real shock!

It was so very unexpected for all of us! Even though I had told most of the people at work that I would be getting married (but didn't know when), each one started screaming when I told them!

Several of my friends have actually wept tears of joy and thankfulness!!! God is so GOOD to use our lives to touch people's lives and increase their faith in God, which is why He allows things like this to happen!!! Every time I read of someone who is hurting over a wounded marriage, it now just comes naturally for me to pray a mighty blanket of God's healing hands to be placed over them and to step forward to minister to them.

At first, we wanted to just go to a Justice of the Peace and get married immediately, but our children said we should have a nice wedding. When I thought about it, I had to agree—these "restoration weddings" need to be a public witness to the mighty power and goodness of our wonderful God—He gets ALL the credit and glory!!!

Yes, of course, like everyone else, I bought most of Erin's videos, and all of her books, which all helped to put me in the right frame of mind. Over the past seven years, God brought me to a place where I had to literally lean on Him completely. He takes each of us on a very unique journey—no two are alike, as Erin said over and over again. So, even though Erin's materials helped me very much to start me out, I learnt not to lean on them, nor on the stories in them, but to completely lean on our wonderful God by just seeking Him and His face and His love every single day!

Did I give up? Oh yes, many, many times. I had to. But almost instantly, God would put something in front of me to bring me back to His way of thinking and back on my journey again. He is so good at turning the heart of all mankind. It's all HIM!!! He is so faithful and good! I praise His wonderful name!!! And may God bless this ministry a hundred fold for every marriage that has been helped!!!

As I said earlier, God changed me by bringing me to a place of total dependence on Him.

I started out very much indoctrinated by "religion." However, He brought me around to His way of doing things!!! :) It is all about relationships, His with us. God changed my situation but nothing was ever really visible, it was entirely spiritually appraised. God taught me two important principles:

1. To take my eyes off my husband and the situation, and to keep them on Him and our relationship.

2. To return good for evil—the single hardest thing that Jesus has asked us to do. It is so powerful but oh so neglected.

From the beginning God gave me the desire for a restored marriage and He kept that desire alive throughout my wait, but to find restoration I had to put it on the back burner. He kept me from dating others even though so many Christians encouraged me there was someone better out there. Imagine.

And, again, it was God who changed me, my heart, my focus and what led to where we are now, remarried! I did not think I needed any changing when my husband divorced me—that was the Pharisee spirit in me alive and well. One of the ladies who helped out at RMI told me that she sensed a Pharisee spirit in me and I was so grateful. It is what helped me to know in order for me to be able to change or I wouldn't have.

Although RMI's materials are excellent, the best you can find anywhere and very, solely Bible-centered, near the end of my journey, I realized I had to learn not to rely on them, but instead on God alone, just as Erin says!! Coming from a very strict "religious" background, it was so easy to fall into relying on RMI, because RMI "had the answers." I had to learn—only God has all the answers I need! I had to pull back from everything and everyone, get closer to HIM, and just TRUST HIM THAT HE ALWAYS KNOWS WHAT HE'S DOING and the reason we are going through this is to know Him!!! :)

~ *Joan in California*

Chapter 12

Linda

"Behold, I am the LORD, the God of all flesh;
is anything too difficult for Me?"
—Jeremiah 32:27

"Everyday is a Gift"

My husband and I had just celebrated our 20th anniversary when I began to notice things were not quite right. We were going through some very difficult financial times and I wrongly assumed that was why he was not quite himself.

He came in on April fool's Day and told me he was leaving. I was shocked! He had always been the giver in the relationship and he had always seemed to be so crazy about me. I couldn't believe what I was hearing. I immediately began to seek God and knew from the beginning that I was to do whatever it took to restore my marriage.

Unfortunately, I tried to do so in the flesh for about nine months until I found the Restore Ministries' web site. My husband was involved with a women that I would have never imagined in my wildest dreams would interest him at all. She was one of our customer's daughters, a former drug addict.

She had spent time in prison for breaking and entering to support her drug habit and she had abandoned her own three sons. Unknown to me she pursued my husband not only at work, but after we invited her to our church. While I was busy serving, she was taking my place. She basically wanted my life: She wanted my husband, my children and my home.

Of course, when my children rejected her, she quickly began a campaign to separate my husband from his children and grandchildren. She flattered my husband and made promises she couldn't keep. Adultery was a way of life for her and my husband was just one of her many victims just as you explain in your book.

Once I was given this knowledge it let me know that our marriage was in serious danger, and so when I searched for help—I found it! Wow!! As soon as I read the Restore Your Marriage book, it was my new life and I began to live it. I must have read in ten times in a row before I stopped to take a breath.

Though I was living it I knew it wasn't enough. To come against what was coming against me, I began teaching from it and from the Wise Woman workbook too. That's when things started to turn around immediately!

Teaching gave me an opportunity to confess regularly that I was very much a contentious woman. My husband and I were Christians but neither of us was living our faith. Then, by reading the books, having a fellowship in my home, I changed from being contentious to becoming **a gentle and quiet spirit.** I began to try to be like the woman I wanted to be as described in Proverbs 31. Instead of arguments, I began to agree with everything my husband said. This included all the praises he said about the woman he was involved with, agreeing to a divorce and all the outrageous stipulations. Not surprisingly I enjoyed staying up and praying all night and found much comfort in fasting (something I never could bring myself to do). Not only did I wear out your book, I wrote hundreds of Scriptures on cards and relied solely on God's Word, constantly, until I could humbly quote the scriptures in my spirit 24/7.

At one point I began praying God's Word out loud and that is when my friends and grown children noticed the change in me. They say it first, and then my husband began to notice. Soon my husband started to call and came by more and more often just to see me.

By following and obeying nearly every principle in the restore book, I was "blessed" when God allowed a second woman to come in to my husband's life, and through her, I knew then that I'd have to obey completely in order to see my restoration come. That's when I realized obedience was just the beginning of my journey, the Lord wanted to be my first love and when I finally got that, things began to change in my heart and I no longer began to care about restoration! Imagine that!

That's when God was free to work on my husband. I realized that as long as my heart was knit to him, the Lord would not touch him. My husband and I were well known and respected in our community. We were also very well off and well thought of. But due to my husband's adultery, like you say in your books, we began to get into a terrible financial condition. During our journey, we were about to lose everything: our business and with it our financial troubles had legal implications. We should have lost our new home, but by God's grace and mercy, the bank didn't want our house!! I knew it was God and God alone!!

We won two of our legal battles, but my husband was sentenced to two years in prison because he had signed a false banking statement. Looking back, God was so good through all of this: we had sown bad seeds for years and were reaping the consequences. Not only was my husband in trouble, but one of our daughters who had never given us any trouble was pregnant and my grown son was battling a serious drug addiction.

Many times I thought my husband was coming home and would panic because at this point I was so content with my life with the Lord as my Husband and first love. Thankfully each turned out to not be the Lord's timing with His will for my life.

It was right after Thanksgiving that my husband asked the second OW to move out. He came to our house the day before he went to be sentenced (he had kept his sentencing a secret from me – clearly God's way to protect me!), and while here he told me five times that morning he loved me!

He hadn't said that in years! It wasn't until I had no feelings for him, only for the Lord, would I hear what I thought would change my life and make me happy. But I had become happy hearing those same words from the Lord, "Linda, I love you."

That day my husband asked if we could make plans to celebrate Christmas with our kids and grandkids on December 23, which just happened to also be our anniversary. And when I agreed that's when he told me about his court date, which was the next day. I didn't say anything nor try to rescue or lessen the impact it was having on him because I knew better. God had truly changed me into a wise woman once I began ministering to women who were as desperate as I was when I found your site and ministry.

The next when he hadn't called, I knew what had happened, that he had been sentenced and was on his way to prison. From that time until he left in January, things got darker and darker. Though most women in my fellowship couldn't understand why God was not "blessing me" but almost punishing me, having the young new Christians watching helped me focus on doing the right thing. I had more than just myself (and my family) to think about.

The original OW was allowed back in our lives, and my husband ended up spending the holidays with her and her family. He would call late at night and got very angry when I missed his call the last time he tried to call before he left for prison. He even opened a bank account with the other woman and made plans for a future with her. Those who watched were devastated and I have to confess it tried to get me down too. But I continued to trust what God said not what I saw.

Again, things began to get even worse. Shortly after my husband went to prison, my son got arrested for drugs. One Sunday morning while I was driving to take insulin to the local jail for my son, I hit the bottom, my faith gone, and I remember saying: "Lord, look at my life: my son is in jail and my husband is in prison. My life does not really glorify You.

I am obeying and I am teaching other women what You have shown me, but why would they want to do this when they look at MY life?" Then, without Him saying anything to me, I just began to praise him through my tears!!

That very afternoon my husband called and my true restoration began. He asked and I felt led to visit him in prison. That's when he began to write love letters to me— I have close to 200 wonderful letters as proof to what God can do!! In one he asked me to marry him again! Soon after his proposal, our son was given a court ordered to attend a rehab.

It's been three years since my husband and I have been restored—but not just to me, but to the Lord, to our children and also to our grandchildren. And due to his love for the Lord that we share, we are more in love than we have ever been in all of our lives! And what a testimony to all of the ladies I have been teaching for 18 months. Though some left, the ones that remained got to see the glory of God in full force. Now they never grumble about what they are going through or how bad it "looks" because no life could look worse that the way mine looked the more I began helping other women.

When I found Restore Ministries, desperately searching the web for help, I have to tell you that I had nothing to offer God but my mistakes. I was suffering and my family was suffering because of my disobedience and contentiousness that led to my husband being so vulnerable to the seduction of the adulteresses (and not one but two). It's when I realized God could use my mistakes to teach other women that my life really changed. And if I would simply tell them what not to do, what I had done, then God could take this horrible mess I had made and use it for His Glory—and He did!!!!

The most important book every married woman should read is *How God Can and Will Restore Your Marriage*. But once in crisis I also listened to the videos and taught dozens of women out of the Wise Woman. Everyday is such a gift to me due to the women that God has brought in to my life! And because the restoration of my marriage HAS brought glory to God, it has given so much hope to the ladies I've met and with whom I've shared my faith and love for my Savior, who have since began making Him their beloved Husband too!

~ Linda in Oklahoma

Gladys

"Behold, I am the LORD, the God of all flesh;
is anything too difficult for Me?"
—Jeremiah 32:27

"Prison & Heroin—
God Delivered me from Both"

My situation began right away in marriage. Soon after we were married, my husband left me! I will say that now I can see that I was to blame for it! After being alone until I was 40 — I wasn't used to submitting to anyone, least of all someone who was starting life over! After a life in prison, my husband was just finding himself and learning to make decisions, by making a lot of mistakes!

I ran my own business and though of myself as educated and capable. What I really was— was arrogant. This drove my husband so far away from me and caused him to run right back to the streets and drugs, leaving me pregnant, heartbroken and confused. I was hurting so badly, I don't even know how to describe it! My arrogance was slammed into the lowest self-image you could imagine!

My husband would contradict now and says I am not to blame me at all. He would tell you how the world and friends and drugs got him into his mess. He would say it was due to his own brother overdosing on drugs, dying in front of him and his sister also dying in a gruesome manner.

But by the time he left me, my husband was so hooked on a combination of heroine and cocaine he could not get off of it by himself. He was also too ashamed to show himself to anyone. Before she died, I used to ask his sister to drive in the area where he was and just tell me if she saw or heard that he was still alive!

I remember lying on the kitchen floor in the middle of the night because I couldn't sleep — all I could pray were weak and pitiful things, like "God help me" through my sobbing and tears. That's about as pitiful and broken as a person can get! But those prayers were heard, and I watched while God did more than I could even think of or muster to ask!

The only thing I asked God was that I wouldn't have to hear that my husband had died. I was so depressed: I never cleaned my house, and barely dragged myself to work or care for anything! But looking back, and seeing all that I went through I can now say it was all worth it, even though at times I didn't even know why I was alive myself, taking my own life!

What changed was that God had a plan to change me and show me His will. A friend, a good dear sister at my church pushed the "How God Can and Will Restore Your Marriage" book into my hands. (I had been given every single other the other well-meaning advice about leaving him, etc. and books that were sold), but since I picked up that book I tell everyone about RMI! As a matter of fact, I don't think anyone in their right mind should wait for troubles to read that book—I think it should be required reading as soon as you decide you want to get married! After all, God didn't say IF troubles come, He said WHEN troubles come!

My friend became my encouragement partner. She was my partner and all I can say is make no excuses… simply do what it says; it was so important to "listen: to what your book says. Even pastors, friends and family can give the wrong advice!

Trust me, I know. When everyone else is saying that what you're going through is hopeless, find even ONE woman to believe with you! GOD sent my friend to me and there is someone out there who needs help too.

My new encouragement partner and I started doing the "A Wise Woman Workbook" together. And slowly I watched God change MY heart as I came to see how His Word covers all circumstances. This book and the one to restore, tells you what to do in EVERY situation! You are NEVER stranded and alone in your troubles!! If you can't find your answer it is only because you don't want the truth.

The process I confess was long and hard. It was so good to have a friend who God sent me to be patient and listen and encourage me when things were so horribly hard! She has a great line. I hear it in my head all the time. No matter how horrible the situation or what I did to mess it all up when it was going well at all, she would simply say, "It'll all be great!"

After a few weeks, I didn't have to call her, I just say it to myself— "It'll all be great!" I did mess up along the way, many times, all due to me wanting to take things into my own hands. Just know that when things get messed up, it's you trying to do it your way. But if you are humbled under God's hand, and things get tough, it's a great place to be because you are completely in His hands! His hands are so much more capable than our own. He did things better than I ever could have! I wanted to be devious and create situations and do things my way. For instance: create an emergency where my husband would have to call or come home. This just backfired so I finally learned to give it to God and God did it better!

As I was re-learning how to be a wife, I was also pregnant. I had no peace about filing for divorce (like people told me to do), or any of that! My older daughter put it well, she said, "You can leave him and marry someone else, but I won't love that person! (This daughter was born to me as a single non-Christian teenager. I became a Christian when I was pregnant with her.)

Remember that my husband was on the streets 2 states away and like every other woman, I was wondering where and how I could find him?! How would God ever bring us back together if I don't even know where he is? Well, in my case this was God's plan.

God didn't want me around messing things up and getting in His way. By my husband not having me around, it caused his circumstances to worsen and that's when he started to reach out to me! He started calling ME, and he was shocked because instead of the woman who used to scream at him "How could you leave me with a baby coming?" I was calm and just listened. I had a gentle and quiet spirit and soon I became his friend once again!

Things began to get hard, though, as he, like me attempted to "deliver himself." I tried to fix me from my contentiousness and he tried to get himself off the drugs. It got so crazy and we went through an awful lot!

Once I told him to come home and I'd help him, but he wouldn't ever be in that state in front of our two girls. He tried it on his own, then he tried a detox center, and finally it became clear that it would take him going back to jail to get clean.

Many of the times I have been brought through were extremely difficult! The turning point in our restoration came slowly, through the calls and some things God asked me to do to restore my husband's faith in me. My husband asked me to send him money. What? Send a drug-addict money?!? But guess what? I did, out of faithfulness to God only and being obedient to my husband. It took A LOT of prayer to know God was really asking me to do this!!

No, that is NOT my advice to everyone; it was specifically for me to do, and you too if you want your marriage restored. But you have to do it because God tells you. If you do it to make your husband happy with you or to prove anything, you mind as well keep your money. The good thing was that I didn't have any money, and then suddenly the Lord blessed me with extra money from my tax return that I wasn't supposed to get.

I knew what the money was for, so I was able to obey after seeking God again and again with scriptures to affirm my action. I wouldn't encourage anyone else to do this, it is important that we don't walk in someone else's story.

Always seek God before moving in ANY direction! It was hard to do. An act of shear obedience to what I was asked to! This was just one lesson I had to go through to learn obedience in the face of many really hard things like that!

God used my obedience in giving my husband this money for good! I had receipts for the money, which ended up being useful in court later! Who knew? God that's who!! We were able to prove that he was not selling drugs, but that I had sent him the money! Now after that experience I know that whatever I am asked to do by God — which is to obey God by being submissive to my husband — I can do and He will work it for good! I am trusting the Lord, not a drug addict husband like everyone accused me of doing. And it wasn't being stupid— it was faith.

Would you believe I even told God once a long time ago that I would never marry anyone with drugs in their past, and to think of it as heroin, that is too strong a drug to ever get over! But when I married my husband, he had not done drugs before, but picked it up after we were married!! Yet God used what I said I would never go through and He used it for my good! God showed me HIS power in that He can restore ANYONE from ANYTHING.

It was many months when finally I knew God was saying it was time to go see my husband. I had wanted to all along, to go see him alive and get "help" for him. But God didn't confirm that to me and so I waited. I finally knew it was going to take him going to jail, and eventually that was where he eventually did go. And talk about using something bad for good—God has used my husband's jail term to restore us completely—even stronger than before! My husband is amazed that I waited and saved his family for him!

Most guys in jail around him have lost everything and there is no one waiting; they realize that they may never see their kids again!! My husband gets to see me and his girls every other week and we all love him so much!

Our visits were always behind glass, which meant he could never hold his new little girl as a baby since he has years still to serve.

When we saw each other for the first time I had this feeling for this man, I knew I belong to this man behind bars, that God told me that he is my husband and must remain my husband! Later my husband told me how he had similar feelings, and we knew God spoke to his heart the same as he spoke to mine. Seeing the change in me, he asked for his own book so I had "A Wise Man Workbook" sent to my husband for his Christmas present! I can only send certain things to jail, so I drew him a picture of the book and you're your ministry send the book to him that he uses to help the men there who also want their families back.

God gave my husband back to me alive and well and believing in God himself! And a man who know talks about Jesus to everyone!! He said he is ready and can't wait to be a husband to me for the rest of his life once he is released!

None of this was easy; God has used this experience to teach me OBEDIENCE — to God and to my husband, nothing I believed in or knew I needed to do! Through this I have learned FAITH in ALL circumstances! I also learned that God loves me; He cares about everything in our lives, and can do ALL things, not just the easy things but the impossible things. Now the power of HIS WORD, of prayer, and praise is real to me. I have confidence and people can see my testimony and come to ME for advice! I know now what is true — if I have read it in God's Word... it is truth!

PRAISE HIM, PRAISE HIM, PRAISE HIM!

Thank you for opening your heart and teaching me the Word. Thank you Erin because what you have shared has opened my blinded eyes. God has done so much by giving your life to helping us!

~ Gladys, RESTORED in Florida

————————Chapter 14————————

Terry

"Behold, I am the LORD, the God of all flesh;
is anything too difficult for Me?"
—Jeremiah 32:27

"Ministry Mixed with Alcohol & Adultery"

My husband has been gone for 3 years due to alcohol and adultery. He had been a pastor for 15+ years before his fall. But it was during this time that God began to show me my failures and all I needed to do. To start with, I was the contentious wife.

Today I knew I needed to write because this week my husband has reentered our family! He has suddenly cancelled the divorce and wants to reconcile!! Our separation has been very public because of the pastorate, but God had set it up this way in order to put our restoration front and center even though it was something our entire family wanted to hide from. In just two days He has begun to pour His healing oil over our lives and it's just so wonderful!

Even I'm a little unsure of the steps to take next, GOD isn't! I believe He will direct both of us because it is very complicated! Right now I am devouring your wise woman book. And today I received an unexpected amount of money and I know it was so I could send this as an offering of praise to the Lord, and in thankfulness to a faithful, faithful God who led me to you!

As you may already know, we have been married for 25 years, but most of it was a very painful time. We spent the past 15 years in ministry, being pastors of many small churches, and it was just three years ago when it all came crashing down.

I knew my husband had been drinking off and on our whole marriage. Then he got heavily involved in pornography, which probably is what led to the adultery. It was then they found out that the church removed him when it was all exposed, and that's when the church sent him away for treatment. We never chose to separate, as church leaders the decision was made for us. And even though people were happy (and I was too) that he was sent to three treatment centers, he was later kicked out of every one of them.

No matter what happened, I was determined to hold it all together and publicly stood (silently) with my husband, at the church we were pastors of, and then again in our small town before all the religious people who mocked our family, saying we would never be healed from this. I rallied with our kids and we prayed for Dad's freedom and deliverance. In the end I had to sell my home, and move into a rental house alone without my husband. I also went back to work and began to be both Mom and Dad to my kids.

After two years of separation while in these treatment centers, he came back to our town attempting to mend our home. It all fell through as he fell into adultery again, and actually moved into the home of a drug addict. The adultery, this time, was very public and the kids and I tried to deal with the pain and shame. People cheered us to go on and dump this man! And if that were not enough, I was warned by many authorities not to allow the kids to see him as he was living in such deception and sin. I was told again and again that the environment was not safe for the kids, and that's what caused a huge amount of anger on his part, and when he filed for divorce.

I was devastated! I had stood by him when others wouldn't and in the end he blamed me. I was then court ordered to attend "parenting after divorce" classes. And it was in that class that a woman gave me your web site and information! Praise God for His timing!! I was at a legal and spiritual crossroads and was seeking God's intervention to know what to do. That night I took the information home and devoured it, and then I ordered the Membership packet of resources. God used Erin's books to open my eyes to the real truth. Though my husband and I were ministers, I had been blinded for 25 years!! First, I was blaming my husband for the sins in our marriage! Now, for the first time I could see the light!! Reading Erin's books and due to my repentance was the turning point of my restoration!

As I sought the Lord, He showed me that, believe it or not, I was the problem... not my husband!! I WAS the contentious woman described in Proverbs and my husband would rather live on the corner of a roof! Unfortunately that is where my husband was now living. I repented before God and wrote a letter asking my husband to forgive me for my sins.

In the past I always tried to "fix him" and not once did I look at me. Believe it or not, the letter was returned to me unopened with a stamp that it was "unable to deliver." I knew the address was correct, but I also knew God's timing and His plan was crucial.

Later God revealed why I wasn't supposed to contact my husband. I made an "exception" to what you teach since my situation, I felt was so different than most. And little did I know it was right when I was trying to contact my husband that my husband had gotten in a fight with the other woman! Not only that but he got a DUI and spent a weekend in jail. Then he had his license taken away and his car impounded. When he came back to his rental room—he contacted me.

He told me he had found a strong church and had enrolled in a Freedom in Christ retreat weekend. During that retreat the Lord set him free from the deception! The blinders came off, and he called **me** crying. I told him about my letter, and he said that he forgave me and that's when he shared about the timing of my letter had it come when I wanted to send it.

The next day, he got a ride to our city and came to our house and showed the kids the legal document that he was canceling the divorce and going to ask God to restore our marriage! We all hugged in the kitchen and he prayed, "Lord heal me. Heal my wife, heal my son, heal my daughter. Heal our home."

The very same week that my husband called to meet with me that he had cancelled the divorce and moved home was the same week you assigned me an ePartner!

I know it was God's timing for my husband to be able to move home once I learned that I cannot fix anyone—not me, not my husband and not our marriage! Now, I lay myself down every day before the Lord for HIM to heal me and change me and restore me. HE is the one who can and will do it for all of us!! *Terri in Minnesota, RESTORED*

Now for the rest of my testimony…

Four years after our restoration, my husband went out drinking one night—took the car my 17 year old son was driving—(my husband had lost his license again) and he was picked up and got another DUI, which resulted is his going to jail.

The good news is that this is what my husband needed to change and the change I guess is going to take about a year. The court says he will be given at least a year in jail; we will know for sure in about 3-5 weeks while he waits for sentencing.

Once again I am choosing to stand strong amidst a lot of public humiliation. This time my own family has turned their backs on me. They say only if I divorce him will they support and rally for me. But, if I decide to stand by him—I will do it alone.

But I know I am not alone! I have a faithful God! I am going to stand and see His salvation once again. God gave me this promise that proves this was necessary to heal our entire family and have room to make the changes in my husband (and of course more in me).

"'The **latter** glory of this house will be greater than the **former**,' says the LORD of hosts, 'and in this place I will give peace,' declares the LORD of hosts" Haggai 2:9.

God told me He needed to restore every bit of our marriage and our home. He has led me to go to the jail to see my husband as much as I can, and my husband also calls everyday so we pray over the phone together.

~ Terry in Minnesota

Ministry Note: Terry is not alone. Often after a restoration God has to get the attention of the husband just like He got with us. Not surprisingly to me any more, but there have been MANY men who have found themselves in jail AFTER restoration to complete the work that sometimes only comes through this kind of refining!

---Chapter 15---

Alesia

"Behold, I am the LORD, the God of all flesh;
is anything too difficult for Me?"
—Jeremiah 32:27

"We Remarried Suddenly!!"

I always thought we had a good marriage. Yeah, we had our arguments and moments of heated discussions, but I always felt we were grounded: no, not in the Lord, but in our own makings. Then on May 9th just one month before our 25th wedding anniversary, I found out that my husband was seeing someone else!

We had become somewhat distant over several months, but I put that blame on our jobs and lack of time together. I was totally devastated and couldn't believe it when I found out. For several weeks I flailed about; I didn't know what to do. I began praying and thinking that I had no right to go to the Lord when I had been so disobedient in the first place, but I was raised in a Christian home and knew who the Lord was, so I felt I had gotten what I deserved.

After many days of crying, not eating, and wondering what I would do, I met a lady that introduced me to RMI. I truly believe the Lord placed this lady in that office that day, just so I would have a place to seek help! You see, the Lord had been trying for **years** to get me back into His fold and I always said "later."

Two months after I met this woman and your ministry, my husband moved out and two months after he moved out our divorce was finalized. I just "knew" it wouldn't go through because I trusted God to stop it, but when it did go through I had to come to terms with that and I had to learn about God's will and why He "let's" things happen we want Him to stop.

Because I never thought of myself as divorced, I refused to tell anyone that we were. Only a few people knew, which I learned later was a good thing. I could hardly say or write the word "divorced" because you see, divorce was never an "option" for me. I never realized that it is an option that our spouses have and it is an option for God to allow for many reasons.

The way God eventually would be able to changed me was for me to come to the realization that I had many things within myself to work out, and one was that somewhere over the years I started taking my husband for granted. He showed me that the remedy to everything was simply by giving the Lord my marriage and circumstances. That He was the only One who was able to restore what my husband and I had destroyed.

Then, from there, as I truly started reading His Word and learning what the Lord expected from me as His bride, a wife, a mother and as a teacher of younger women, I became content in knowing that the battle was already won. My husband would be home as soon as the Lord was done with ME.

The other thing I learned was about fasting and the right kind of praying and the importance of these things in my life. I often prayed, but never really interacted with the Lord. I used prayers for asking for what I wanted and I never even thought or cared about His will or how He longed for a real intimate relationship with me. And due to this, I realize that it was only a matter of time before God would need to get my attention, which thankfully He did!

God began to change my situation slowly but surely as I sought the Lord. No I didn't see my situation improve with my husband, but I started seeing changes not just in me, but also in my husband as the Lord started turning his heart.

Not right away of course, but slowly. Each time I got closer to the Lord, He saw fit to move my husband closer to Him and then ultimately to me.

It was amazing how the Lord also saw to it that I heard from my husband at just the right times. Before I let go and made the Lord my Husband (not just when I said it but my life reflected it), I never saw or heard from my husband, which was always my greatest fear. Now that we were divorced and not connected in anyway, I was afraid if I didn't make contact or if I truly let go as the ministry tells us to, then he would be gone forever.

Yet just as they also say, as soon as I did let go completely, then it didn't matter, and that is when He was able to show me how much in control He was. He not only allowed my husband to see occasionally, accidentally when I lease expected it. But more importantly, due to these being unplanned it allowed my husband to see me for who I had become and what I had to offer: my love and forgiveness, which I had withheld (before coming to this ministry) in order to hurt him.

Though I never said anything, after learning that to win anyone it is without a word, I could sense my husband could see that I cared for him differently. No longer needy, no longer vulnerable, I had all I needed, which became attractive to him.

The key principles God taught me were to remain still and allow the Lord to do all the work—He didn't need my help in turning my husband's heart and He didn't need my help in bringing the OW's true colors to light. God promises those things in His Word, so when we get in and mess around, we are not blessed. I allowed the Lord to do what He alone can do, and He did!

Thank God I understood quickly why we are not to pursue or call our spouses— that they need to be completely removed from our hearts!! It's His means of protecting us and protection is something we need during this trial or we will give up and be discouraged. God will protect, but only if we don't let our emotions guide our actions and we go against or reject what you teach us we are supposed to do (all which is based on Scriptures).

There were many difficult times God brought me through by carrying me. One, I recall, was very early on, before finding your ministry, so my heart was still very tied to my husband. My husband was going to a school out of state and I realized that he was leaving earlier than he needed to and I knew he was leaving and making a stop out of his way. Though he never mentioned visiting the OW, I didn't need to ask. And though he was always very good about keeping in touch with me through the whole time we were apart up until this point, while on this trip, he never called once. He told me he just "needed time to himself." However, I knew in my heart that he was with her and I spent lots of time crying to the Lord for strength and comfort. Not only did He use it to break me so that I would let go, He blessed me double and gave me wonderful ladies to pray with and begin to minister with. Praise God for these ladies!!! These were the ladies who began meeting together in order for us to grow in the Lord. Now our Home Fellowship meets weekly and we introduce new women to RMI ever week!

The turning point of my restoration started in late November. My husband was still torn between coming home and the OW, but thankfully I too was torn. I wasn't sure I wanted restoration, and I believe this had a huge impact on who my husband finally did choose.

In January he moved to Texas (just a 12-hour drive from us) because he's in the military. That move, though closer to us, also meant he was able to see the OW more often. And that gave him opportunities to see the bitterness emerging in this woman. And that's when he realized that he wanted to have his family back and we made plans to remarry.

My decision about who to choose came from God emphasizing His will, not our own, and also about thinking of others as more important than ourselves or our desires. About laying down our lives for our friends, and by now my husband and I were friends again. My husband wanted to do the right thing, and for me not to accept would have been putting my desires over his.

My restoration actually happened in February when my husband called and said he felt he needed to drive home so that we could be remarried two days later! Wow!!

I wasn't sure I was ready for it to happen that quick! What an unexpected call and how suddenly it all happened. He actually called to see I would be willing to get married again the day he called. And though I still wasn't sure, God made the way for it to happen. So God brought forth a suddenly in my restoration just as you said it would happen once my priorities were right!! As soon as I honestly didn't want restoration, but I wanted only Him, it began to happen.

How I found your site from "an angel sent from our Lord" and now wonderful friend who took time to look for hurting women like me even though she was going through things much worse that what I was going through. And after you knew the Lord was first in my life and I would only call on Him when I was in need and lean only on Him, I was given a wonderful e-Partner and even to this day, years later, we still communicate. I can't imagine not having these ladies from our fellowship in my life now. By pouring out, God continues to pour into me. Not only do I recommend all of your resources to everyone I meet, women who don't live by me I guide in the direction of your website and have heard they too have been amazingly changed and many restored. I believe that my restoration happened because I finally learned "the basics" of how to be the woman God created us to be. To be His bride and only then to be the sort of wife, mother, and teacher the world around us needs. But most of all, I want to thank you for leading us all to the Lord, who is great, and is worthy of our love.

~ Alesia in Alabama, RESTORED

Chapter 16

Sabrina

"Behold, I am the LORD, the God of all flesh;
is anything too difficult for Me?"
—Jeremiah 32:27

"RESTORED After Falling into Adultery with my Ex-Husband"

Hello and may God blessed you with the desires of your heart as you begin to follow the Lord and His plan for your life.

My name is Sabrina and I'm 43yrs old and I have 4 grown children. What brought me here to this ministry was because God saw my heart that was full of sorrow and hurts. However through my separation, which led to divorce (and I was the one who filed the divorce), my heart bled for years and I could not understand it. But I ended up back with my former husband after all those years of separation, because I began to follow His ways. It was then God started my Restoration Journey and I began my journey.

Here is my RESTORED Marriage TESTIMONY.

I always had in my heart that I wanted to marry someday, but, I never knew that I actually would. When I met my husband I knew there was something special about him. I had always been very shy when I dated, but not with him. We began dating and my husband surprised me one day by making a statement saying, "You are going to be my wife."

I knew there was something about him, but marriage wasn't what I had in mind and from my expression he knew it too. As we were dating, GOD started dealing with us in regards to intimacy, since we were not married. We started reading a book that "scared us straight" and we quickly married and began going to church.

After 3 years we started having troubles and I became contentious. I constantly started asking him to leave and also began shaming him by my words, which resulted in him becoming distant. I just didn't care anymore! Satan had a field day with me and boy did I suffer because of it! You guessed it! My husband just up and left me. We were separated for 5 years and after 3 ½ years, I wanted a divorce, even though a "still small voice" was telling me not too. But because I was rebellious, I went through with the divorce that my husband never wanted. Afterwards like most of you, I felt empty and lonely, so I began dating a married man (who was at the time separated) thinking it was going to help me to get my husband out of my heart and off my mind. But GUESS WHAT???? It didn't.

I can honestly tell you that I really don't know how I ended up here at RMIEW, but thank God I did. This ministry has brought me such a long way and has showed me so many things I never knew about. It's a wonderful place to be and to grow in the Lord and experience Him, believe me I know!

Now over the years I always told God I wished He would fix my marriage, and wanted to know why I could not get my ex husband out of my heart. This is something I just couldn't understand. I cried for so long and then soon after coming here I ran into him. I found out he was involved with someone else and had been with this woman for 4 and a half years (she was married but separated from her husband).

After seeing him, I realize I wanted my marriage back and then stopped messing with the man I was with. My husband, on the other hand, was still involve with the other woman so it looked pretty hopeless. As I said, I guess I always wanted my marriage and felt that is it hopeless until I ran across your ministry.

I quickly read Erin's book How God Can and Will Restore Your Marriage and boy did this show me so many things about myself and what I could finally admit, that the marriage mess was my fault. I felt so hurt because of my past actions. But reading Erin's testimonies and all the others made me feel wonder and hopeful that possible mine could be restored too.

Soon God began helping me a lot, but I realized I needed someone to be there to guide me. I knew it would not be easy. Soon after I changed, I began to see my ex and talk to him, but knew this was not enough. I wanted to see God move just like he moved in Erin's situation and everyone else's. When I filled out my questionnaire I ended it with: Please help me.

Thankfully I never went to counseling, so I didn't make mistakes like that. On Friday, December 23, 2011, was a big turning point for me, it's when I decided I needed to begin helping other woman, and I filled out the Minister in Training Evaluation so I knew what I would need to learn to help women in crisis.

RMI has meant so much to me. When I applied to become a Minister in Training I wrote to the Team:

My heart is so still so overwhelmed because of things I have learn about myself. It has made such a difference in me, because I didn't know I was carrying all this stuff. It's been a challenge but what you all mean to me, words can't express. You all have help me to see what God has probably been trying to show me but I couldn't sit still long enough to listen. You showed me it's not all about me and my marriage being restored, but it's more about helping others— thank you so much!

The reason I am interested in becoming a MITC "Minister in Training Candidate" is that even though I never thought of being a minister, I know I can encourage other women very well, even when I can't encourage myself. There have been many people who tell me that I needed to be a minister, but I thought "No, not me." But I really enjoyed just lifting people up, you know, it made me feel better when I did.

NOW, after being here almost a month, and going through your first course, I now want to be what GOD wants me to be, and if it's being a minister, wow, it will be such a joy to know you made a difference in one person life—that's joy! When Jesus healed the ten lepers and only one came back, it make me look at myself. I want to be the one who came back and made the difference.

Now I need to confess that with all of this I tripped up! My husband continued to come to see me after seeing the changes in me, and we continued to see each other **but against scripture,** we started having sexual relations even though we were divorced. Deep down inside I knew it was wrong, which only led my husband to be confused between me and the other women. Then he left me again after 3 months after he had promised we were would marry. I was devastated.

Surprisingly, this time I was okay, and knew I just needed more time with the LORD. I went through storm after storm, but God was always with me. I confessed my involvement with my FH to the RMIEW leaders, and I was immediately set free from guilt. Then I began to move forward and put all my focus on the Lord—completely letting go of my husband. I kept my mouth quiet, fasted and constantly prayed to be closer to Him. That's when He helped me learn to depend on Him and Him alone.

It was at this time that I wanted even more to help other women with marital issues because I didn't want anyone to feel the way I was feeling. I wanted to share the peace I received after I finally put God first in my life and began seeking Him alone; not my husband or my children. I started trusting Him in everything because He wanted so much to be part of every situation my life (as well as yours).

The turning point came when my ex-husband and I began dating him again but I also found out about the OW, that she was still in my husband's life. I cried like never before to GOD, pouring my heart out to Him. I started talking to GOD and I told Him how I was feeling (not anyone else) and that I wasn't going to stop crying out to Him and He helped me.

As I said before, He first led me to find Restore Marriage Ministries and I knew it was GOD's will to restore my marriage after I saw the heading "How God Can and Will Restore Your Marriage." I ordered the book and discovered God's principles, and I learned how I had violated so many of them, which brought me to my KNEES. I immediately asked God to forgive me and went to all five of my children and confessed my faults instead of my husband's faults as I had done in the past. Then I was led to contact my former husband and apologize for everything. HE said that he had forgiven me a long time ago. Ladies, God is AWESOME! I first would like to thank God for what He is doing in my life and KNOW this; I had nothing to do with this. NOTHING!

On March 8, 2013, my marriage was restored! YES it really! MINE! I was **remarried** on March 8th and believe it or not. Just before we remarried, my husband began opening up his heart to me and spending time with me but this time without us being intimate—I just couldn't believe he wanted to wait too. WOW! God knows how to turn things around!!!

My husband even apologized and confessed that he never wanted to leave me. I can't express enough how long I was not ready for all of this and why I asked the Lord if it is His will and He if wanted us to be remarried, then have my husband ask me again—and to my amazement—he did! Yes, I still have a lot of work to do, but my GOD has got me. Ladies God is AWESOME and He is all we need.

Dear friend, never think the Lord doesn't hear your cries, He does. We can't help, but God is faithful in every area you need Him in. You see, this is why you are here now because He's heard you cry. Be ready to grow and know that everyone in this ministry loves and cares for you.

"Dear Jesus, guide and help this woman and let her know that, there's nothing to impossible for You and You are their new Husband now and trust You only. AMEN". Be Blessed.

~ Sabrina in Georgia

Chapter 17

Dawn

"Perfect love casts out fear…
and the one who fears
Is not perfected in love."
—1 John 4:18

"Coming Full Circle"

As I was sitting in church recently with my husband and children, listening to the preacher, God reminded me that we were in this same place two years prior, but with a broken marriage. God truly has brought everything full circle. As the preacher continued his sermon, I remembered being at the very same altar two years ago asking the Lord to please give me peace and to show me what I needed to do. I had no idea that everything that would transpire afterward would be for my own good—for I was nowhere near the kind of Godly woman that the Lord needed me to be.

I was not serving the Lord the way I was supposed to be serving Him. I was neither hot nor cold, but lukewarm. I was comfortable going to church and trusting God for things. However, I was not on fire for Him. I did not take pleasure in nurturing the ministry the Lord gave me (my family) through cooking, cleaning, and other household duties. I did not allow my husband to be the leader of our family. I did not listen nor respect him. I was clean on the outside, but filthy on the inside, and I didn't even know it. I was gradually tearing my house down until my life and marriage ended up going down into sinking sand.

While deep in the sand, I humbled myself and prayed to the Lord and repented of my sins. I asked the Lord to make me a better wife to my husband. In my cries to the Lord, He had one of my friends send me the link to How God Can and Will Restore Your Marriage, and my eyes began opening wide to the kind of woman I truly was and how I needed to be. I was disobedient to God's Word — rebellious, contentious, and a Pharisee. Though I asked my husband to forgive me, he already decided that he wanted a divorce and planned to move out of the house as soon as he could. Yet, I knew God would restore my marriage, despite how things appeared, and continued to hold on to His promises. Although I wanted my husband to stop his thoughts and actions of divorce and turn his heart back to me, I began praying and seeking for God's will in my life.

As I trusted God more and more for His will to be done, He provided me with a complete makeover. He took away the victim coat and showed me that I was actually the perpetrator: I was contentious, hateful, bitter, unforgiving, deceitful and loud. I hated being home. The Lord had a lot of work to do within me. It was painful to look in the mirror and see that I wasn't the person I thought I was, not the person others thought I was. Chaste and respectful, one of the lessons I studied while reading A Wise Woman, I was not. The Lord was gracious enough to show me that I hadn't embodied any of these Godly qualities, and was a harlot in every sense of the word. The Lord removed all of my ugly, worldly traits layer by layer, and replaced them with fruits of the spirit; love, joy, peace, forbearance, kindness, goodness, faithfulness, gentleness and self-control.

All of the biblical principles discussed in the RMI resources I didn't know to begin with, so I had to re-study them multiple times to sink in. The tests that I underwent after learning and studying of His Word were much harder and painful than the ones from my school days, but they are also more rewarding.

I struggled with several things - learning not repaying evil for evil, keeping my mouth shut, and not defending myself. Though difficult, the best part is that the Lord was always with me. He saved me from the fire, and although He may not have always spoken to me in the midst of my testing and trials, He never left me. These tests stretched my faith (especially when I couldn't hear Him) and gave me the endurance that I needed to finish this part of my race.

The most difficult obstacle for me to overcome was fear. The Lord addresses fear many times in His Word. In Isaiah 40:10 NIV, it says "So do not fear, for I am with you; do not be dismayed, for I am your God. I will strengthen you and help you; I will uphold you with my righteous right hand." I clung to my fears - fear of rejection, fear of being hurt again. After the Lord allowed the divorce to go through and He began bringing the wall down between me and my husband and began bringing my husband around, my fear still grew within me and I pushed my former husband away. I pushed him away a few times before the Lord showed me what was happening. He revealed to me that my restoration journey was almost a year longer than it should had because I kept intervening, leaning on my own understanding rather than His. God was putting things back together again, but I was pushing them apart. God was bringing my husband around and allowing my husband to allure me, but I was pushing him away. Once I realized it, I asked the Lord to help me conquer my fear and restore my marriage if it truly was His will.

In His will for my journey, I ended up going through the seasons with the Lord as my Husband twice, due to my fears. The second time around, I learned to relate to every situation and everyone on a different level than before. Each season gave me a deeper appreciation for the Lord as my Husband. While I was going through the seasons with my Love, I was also going through the season with my then former husband. I was and am so in love with the Lord that I had let everything go, but He kept telling me that a life of singleness (as defined by the world) was not His will for me and my children.

The turning point in my journey came about when my former husband continued alluring me, and this time I knew what it was - God's will. We were in Canaan Valley, ironically, when the Lord told me that despite my mistakes and fears that He was going to restore my marriage. Wow! There were hints hidden in different things the Lord was showing me. After the Lord's revelation to me, my former husband and I talked even more, but all appeared to stay the same.

Then my friend passed away. I was devastated! I watched his marriage get restored not even a month before he died. During this time, my former husband was there to comfort me and my daughter. The Lord used this sorrowful time in my life to bring us even closer together and make our relationship new.

The thought of remarriage to my former husband never crossed my mind. I was happy with the Lord as my Husband and very content living the way that we were. However, the Lord had other plans. My husband decided that he wanted us to get remarried as soon as possible and then the Lord took over from there. This was one of my biggest tests in my journey - overcoming my fears of remarriage and trusting in the Lord. The morning of our wedding ceremony, I was so overcome with fear that when the judge commented about never marrying a bride with cold feet, I nearly passed out. I was praying to the Lord during the entire ceremony to help me conquer my fear and keep obedient to His will; I wanted to run. He reminded me of 1 John 4:18 (NASB) which says that "there is no fear in love, but perfect love casts out fear because fear involves punishment, and the one who fears is not perfected in love." The Lord helped me through the entire ceremony which lasted two minutes, but seemed like an eternity.

There has been a whirlwind of changes that the Lord has made in me. Changes that I could not have made on my own. God has been using me to help others in their Restoration Journeys **from the very beginning of mine**.

I always enjoyed helping others in their time of need, which is why I am a volunteer firefighter, and helping others with their journey is an extension and a new part of serving others through and for the Lord. I also love being home and serving my family now. I am learning so many things about being home, cooking and cleaning. I am still getting brave enough to learn how to quilt, sew, and crochet, as I love to learn. Although I am a work in progress, I am content with being at home and taking care of my first mission field, my family. This is something I always wanted to do, but didn't know how until I was led to this ministry.

Now I am starting a new part of this journey with new tests and trials. I am so glad that I had RMI and all of their resources to help me be ready for this part of the journey.

I know that this is a lifelong journey and the thing that I want everyone to know is that I love the Lord with all my heart.

I recommend every resource RMI has to offer. They are filled with the truth that every woman coming to this ministry needs. I read all of them at least twice, and keep them for future reference. I also suggest writing out the Bible verses that speak to your heart on 3X5 cards. The resources are so wonderful and give you the raw truth while you are broken to help you build a relationship with the Lord as your Husband.

When I found RMI, I was broken and looking for the truth. I found this ministry just when I needed it, which confirms that the Lord's timing is perfect. I couldn't take the RMI courses right away so I reread what I did have from the ministry, and then moved on to other books like workers@home about keeping up with my home — another part of His plan.

During this journey, which will last for a lifetime, I found something I never had before, a real relationship with the Lord. When He took me as His bride, my life completely changed. Things that used to matter to me no longer mattered. I wanted and want to live to please Him, and do the things He called me to do.

Honestly, I would not change a single minute of the time I spent getting to know my new Husband. It was time that I needed with Him. He is still my everything and now that I obey Him and have a restored marriage as a result. He has been blessing me so much that I cannot even begin to tell you in just a testimony or praise report. He has given me back everything that I lost over the past two years ago—and so much more. Everything that I allowed the enemy to steal from me since I never tithed and was ignorant to the truth.

I hope that each of you all find Him in a deeper more intimate way, a relationship with Him is worth every tear, heartache, and loss that you will endure.

God's plan is to bring everything full circle as we follow Him along our Restoration Journey.

~ Dawn in Ohio

Chapter 18

Sonnette

"So do not fear, for I am with you;
do not be dismayed, for I am your God.
I will strengthen you and help you;
I will uphold you with my righteous right hand."
—Isaiah 40:10 NIV

"Better for Me Then, than now"

"Remarrying My Earthly husband"

My praise report today is based on today's Daily Encourager, "Where Would I be Without Your Love", because I have been so encouraged by it. I cannot allow the enemy to steal the joy of what God is busy doing in my life right now.

"Through the praise of children and infants you have established a stronghold against your enemies, to silence the foe and the avenger." Psalm 8:2

I have been thinking about what to write in my PR but have been putting it off thinking I would write my PR after my vows have been said, yes ladies you read correctly, my remarriage to my earthly husband   is at hand and I Praise God and give Him the Glory!!!

"Do not conform to the pattern of this world, but be transformed by the renewing of your mind." Romans 12:12

"If anyone is in Christ He is a new creation; the old has gone, the new has come!" 2 Corinthians 5:17

"Be made new in the attitude of your minds; and put on the new self, created to be like God." Ephesians 4:23-24

What I would like to encourage you ladies about today is this: Don't be afraid to leave behind the old self, the old mindsets (thoughts), the friends, the family, in-laws, and embrace being alone with the Lord making Him your heavenly Husband and allowing Him to be Your Husband, Provider, Comforter and Strength.

Do not be conformed by the pattern of this world but be transformed by the renewing of your mind. This verse resonated through me after feeling so far away from the Lord during a 3-day fast, and after SG, He showed me that I needed to have His Word stored in my heart and mind, that I needed His Word to fill me up and be my focus. So it was back to my 3 x 5 cards to not only read, but this time to memorize. When we have God's Word filling up our hearts and minds, the enemy can't steal our joy in the Lord!

Ladies, I want to encourage you, many, many PR of Restored Marriages are at hand!! Stay focused on the Lord, make Him our heavenly Husband and given Him the First place in our lives. When my earthly husband and I were dating, he used to tell me that "I'm perfect for him". I wondered if I would ever hear those words said to me again. Well I did ladies! :), and for this I can only give the Lord the highest Praise!

"I am still confident of this: I will see the goodness of the Lord in the land of the living. Wait for the Lord; Be strong and take heart and wait for the Lord." Psalm 27:13-14

At RMI we are taught Revelation 2:4, "For I have this against you, you have left your first love." I am certain that this restoration journey will always and forever be a success when we "delight ourselves in the Lord" and we know that "He will give us the desires of our hearts"!!! :) :) :)

"RESTORED in South Africa"

It all began in February 2012, a couple of days after our 7-year anniversary. My sister-in-law came to tell me that my husband was involved with another woman and that a year prior had been involved in a relationship I knew nothing about.

Sadly, I handled the situation all wrong from day one! Of course, I was devastated and heartbroken and had a feeling of unbelief like (IS THIS REALLY HAPPENING TO ME???). Unfortunately, like so many women do, I confronted my husband and the OW at their workplace as they worked together, and just continued to handle the situation all wrong by snooping, asking questions and confrontations.

Of course, my situation only got worse and worse and a month or two later my husband asked me to move out and find a place for my daughter and I to live, while. He moved in with the OW. And because I continued to pursue him and again confronted the OW, the OW forced my husband to divorce me. During all of this I was seeking the Lord and I became a part of the "Stander's Ministry", but there was a lot I still did not know and had to learn, but the Lord did give me peace regarding the divorce.

God did start changing me as I started growing closer to Him due to the heartache I was experiencing seeing my husband with another woman.

As I desperately prayed, things started getting bad between my husband and the OW and a couple of months later their relationship came to an end and my husband moved in with me (but we were divorced) and it caused my contentiousness to worsen. I snooped on my husband's cell phone and found a pic of him with a new OW and that's when he moved out and in with a friend.

At that time, I became heartbroken again, my heart felt like it had broken into a million pieces. I cried out to the Lord in desperation asking Him why? Why was I having to go through the pain and heartache of another OW, this was the third time— I could not understand! I thought after my husband moved in I was "experiencing" a restored marriage. It was at this time I truly believe the Lord heard my desperate prayers and led me to a woman who posted a prayer request on a website and sent me the RYM book. This was the turning point and from the time I read the RYM book!

Reading RYM is when I started understanding and started experiencing a peace that surpasses all understanding. God's Word says that we shall know the truth and the truth shall set us free, but I up until the point of reading the book, I was being destroyed for lack of knowledge.

God taught me to forgive, especially in the beginning when I found out about the OW, this was an area I prayed a lot about and it was not easy but I knew I had to. Now looking back, I thank God because I now realize the new OW that entered my husband's life was a chance for me to put into practice the principles I learned from the RYM book and a test for me to again work on my contentiousness and letting go.

After reading RYM, I also completed the Free Marriage Evaluation Questionnaire and received the Daily Encourager with it's amazing testimonies of women going through similar situations. I was sent the lesson regarding "Intimacy when Divorced" and I started my first lessons with RMI.

Ministry Note: Stander's ministries encourage women who are divorced to be intimate with their husbands, which is why his moving back, after they were divorced, made Sonnette believe she had experienced a restored marriage.

When I came to RMI another important principle I learned was tithing, since embracing this principle and tithing here to my storehouse, I have not suffered lack, not a day went by that my daughter and I did not have what we needed!

When I was without a job (another Praise as I started a new job in the same week I got remarried to my husband), I did not lack as whenever I was really low on funds and would not even have money for bread— my heavenly Husband would always provide for us in the nick of time! What I learned was that when we tithe He does rebuke the devourer!

The most difficult times that God helped me through was after my husband left the second time (after I believed I had experienced a restored marriage) and we separated again. The very first month I lost a lot of weight and struggled to come to terms with what I was going through. I was very desperate and at that time I did not have such a close relationship with the Lord. In my desperation I asked God for a sign or to show me what I was going through or why I was going through it, anything. On two separate occasions God spoke to me.

The first time was through a vision where He showed me a leg that was full of pus, and the pus had popped and it was healing. Then He showed me a sore, then a scar and then the sore completely healed with no scar. Then on the second occasion God spoke to me through a colleague who told me about a sermon he had watched on T.V. The preacher was preaching about how snow falls on the ground and how it can destroy a crop, but that the destroyed crop is what prepares the soil for the next crop because it destroys all insects and weeds from the soil.

I guess God needed to speak to me in these ways because at that time I was not reading and studying God's Word like I do now through RMI. Now because I read the Bible everyday and do the lessons daily through at RMI, God gave me hundreds and hundreds of promises through His Word that I was reading and studying.

The turning point in my restoration happened when I started reading the "How God Can & Will Restore Your Marriage Book". As I read, God started showing me the areas I needed to repent of that led to the breakdown of my marriage. Applying the "Letting Go" principle and the "Intimacy After Divorce" principle led to HUGE positive and immediate changes!!

I suspected and believed I was close as soon as I started reading the RYM Book and as I started doing the lessons. Being a "Stander," I suffered a lot of setbacks and frustrations where things seemed to be going well, but then something would happen and I would fall to pieces every time. You see my husband and I got along very well. Even when he was living with the OW, we would chat and were quite close. But the missing link was the principles I learned through RMI, which kick started my Restoration Journey to completion!!

I would recommend everything that RMI has to offer: the books, the videos, the Daily Encourager and most of all the Bible. Reading the Bible everyday in conjunction with doing your lessons everyday and praying God's Word, packs a powerful punch! I would also recommend doing the 3 x 5 cards which RMI teaches us to write down and read throughout the day and to also memorize as many promises from God's Word. Hide them in your heart so that the enemy cannot steal God's promises.

I encourage every lady reading this to never, never ever give up!! Just continue to do your lessons daily and if you're not doing them—sign up for lessons! And please don't be just a hearer but be a doer of the Word and do everything that you are taught. You are so very blessed that the Lord has led you here to RMI to teach you the truth of God's Word.

So be sure to hide God's Word in your heart, memorize as many scriptures as you can and always remember that FAITH moves mountains! God is a God of the impossible and He is MORE than ABLE! His word never returns void but ALWAYS accomplishes its purposes!!

"It was Better for Me Then than Now"

It has been a month since I experienced a restored marriage and I have been very happy, my husband and I are so in love. It is everything and more than what my heart desired for a restored marriage. As happy as I am, there has been something missing and I know all too well what it is....

My First Husband. My heart, mind and spirit (in the busyness of work, my home, my husband, my daughter, washing, cooking and tidying) longs for, pants for, my Husband and we both want to get back what I had together: the time alone with Him, speaking to Him, hearing Him speak to me. Once you know THIS awesome HUSBAND you cannot go back.

When you SEEK HIM, He will show you as He showed me. As I read the "What Now" that was sent to me from RMI after submitting my restored marriage testimony. This is what the Lord showed me and it is so funny, LOL, because before I came to RMI I used to pray this same scripture for my then estranged husband, desperately, feverishly— when he was living with the OW!!

Hosea 2:7 "She (I used to put he or my husband) will run after her lovers, but she won't catch them. She will search for them, but she won't find them. Then she will say, 'I'll go back to my first husband. Things were better for me than they are now."

Back then, I used to pray desperately for my husband, praying that as he ran after his lovers he would not find them, that he would look for them and not find them. AND NOW I KNOW.

These scriptures were for me, yes me!! What struck me was these words from the verses above "I will go back to my husband, it was better for me then than now"!

During my time of being divorced, looking back it was "better for me then than now", my relationship with my Husband was idyllic, I lived for Him, I spent so much time with Him. I loved Him and He loved me; it was such a special time, it was glorious, it was marvelous and it was awesome :) :) I loved it!!!!

Ladies, I want to encourage you to enjoy your time with your Husband (while it lasts), because before you know it, if you fall in love with your heavenly Husband and let go of your EH, you will be restored to your earthly husband and long for your time you once had only for Him.

I praise God for showing me how better it was for me then than now, because my attention and focus was Him and how He taught me through RMI to put Him first. "Yet I hold this against you: You have forsaken the love you had at first." Revelation 2:4.

God is so awesome and so in tune with you when you pray, as He shows you great and unsearchable things.

Jeremiah 33:3 "Call to Me and I will answer you and show you great and unsearchable things you do not know."

So I'm happy to run and jump into my Husband's arms, His love is amazing!!

~ Sonnette in South Africa

Chapter 19

JoAnne

"Do not call to mind the former things,
Or ponder things of the past.
I will even make a roadway in the wilderness,
Rivers in the desert."
—Isaiah 43:18-19

"Humble Yourself"

God is good! My husband called one Saturday night around 11:30, clearly upset, and then asked me if I still wanted him. He told me that before I answered, he had to tell me everything. He did tell me everything and I was so sad for him because of the trials he was going through, so much pain.

Due to me learning what to do, God has been protecting me and while this was going on, I was in a peaceful calm place.

It was only 5 hours earlier when I once again completely humbled myself and cried out to the Lord. I cried so hard asking for him to change **me**, guide **me** and to **forgive me** because I had cost my son his father by my angry ways. I don't know everything that I said when I prayed, but I was pouring myself out to the Lord.

I was also looking forward to starting the classes here and thanked him for the material I had already been reading. Later that same night, my husband called and asked to come home. He arrived at home quickly because I found out he was already driving when he called. It seemed as though he was fleeing for his very life!

He left where he was living without saying anything and even left all his belongings (that were with him) there. I also found out that he had packed up weeks **before** to come home, but didn't. He says he wishes he had, but I knew it wasn't the right time because I wasn't fully where I needed to be. God protected me from failing miserably. I also believe that it gave him a more clear picture of his surroundings because on returning home, he said he never wants to live that way again. It was all due to the grace of God and Him answering my prayer, but only when he knew I was humbled enough and was ready.

The reason for my restoration, I know, was because I did seek God that night with my whole heart and soul. I didn't put my marriage first in my prayers, this time, but rather my relationship with Him. I completely and utterly humbled myself before Him like never before. I had also been doing some fasting that entire week. I don't think that my husband would have come home at that moment in time if I hadn't turned myself over to God completely.

How did everything begin? First I started reading all your materials. Then began working through your workers@home book... of which I am still de-cluttering but this is where I started. I had been making sure everything was ready for my husband following what that book was teaching about making my home ready for my husband's return.

And of course, I have been focused on God's lesson of a virtuous wife and following everything I learned. I separated myself from all who did not support me and put my sole focus on my relationship with the Lord only. I also completely stopped emailing my husband and even having the urge to meddle in God's works on him through praying for him. One of the lessons I read a lot, teaches us to really let go, not just say it but completely let go.

I did that and humbled myself, focusing on my relationship with the Lord only. No friends, no family nothing but the Lord (except work). I toiled in my house making it a haven. One of the first things my husband told me is that he really loves what I have done with the house. I was also told how good I smell and that is from the book of Esther that I had been applying in my personal grooming.

The most difficult part of my journey had to be the loneliness as I do not live near family or friends. I moved to this city because of a job opportunity. My husband encouraged me to take it although it was away from him and our sons. I did as he asked, and while I didn't do it consciously thinking, like "I need to submit to him" that is what I did. My husband told me that he had me move here because he wanted us to split up. Then, at the end of December I was given Isaiah 43:18-19 and knew God was building the road in the wilderness to bring my husband home while he sent a river "refreshing" in the desert (where I live) to me. I am here so we can together be refreshed and grow in God's word.

The turning point was when I truly began humbling myself before God and **completely** turning it all over to him. It is having complete faith and demonstrating it by truly letting God deal with my husband. I had to stop meddling in God's work and plan. I wasn't shown this site until mid December and only because it was time to learn the principles of being the person who trusts God in all things.

How it all happened was that my husband just called after not talking to me for 60 days, hanging up on me when I called out of the blue (the day after Thanksgiving). I knew he would call at some point, but I did not expect him to call with such emotions, nor be driving 3 hours to return home leaving all the items he had taken with him. And based on what your resources have done for me, I do give them to people all the time. Recently I shared two of your books with my prayer partner.

To conclude my testimony, I want so say that you **must** give yourself fully over to the Lord. You must **not** dwell on circumstances but **trust Him** in all things. Learn everything you can straight from the bible and keep learning how to be the wife God wants you to be, making your home as He wants it by going through your courses. Remember, in your darkest hours the Lord will answer and shine the brightest if you turn to Him and no one else. Again, give yourself over to Him and watch your miracle happen.

~ JoAnne in Nevada

Chapter 20

Lakisha

"My sacrifice, O God, is a broken spirit;
a broken and contrite heart
you, God, will not despise."
—Ps. 51:17 (NIV)

"Restoration in D.C."

My name is Lakisha and I am from Washington, D.C. I had been married for 9 years as of March 2011, when I became part of a marriage group on Facebook with several other women in marriage crisis and they sent me the book, "How God Can and Will Restore Your Marriage." Soon afterwards, at the end of February 2011, I filled out a Marriage Evaluation Questionnaire.

My restoration journey began after seven years of marriage when I had gotten pregnant with our second child and my husband got bit by what I call "the lust bug." Every woman (or any activities involving women) caught his attention. He stepped out on me several times, disrespected me and was very abusive.

At the end of the seven years, when he decided he needed to treat me better and our three kids, he found out he had another child out of wedlock. He went to court for paternity for this child (who was born on my birthday).

During this trial, the Lord taught me to focus on GOD and work on myself. Stop seeing my husband's sins and faults and get myself together to be a better wife, mother and servant of God.

The transition was not easy and accepting that there was a possibility of another child out there that was not ours together made it worse.

I struggled with accepting that this child was his, and agreed we would have to take custody of her in order to keep her out the CPS system. I prayed and cried and prayed and cried a lot!! I thought this was God's sign to run for the hills. But, after much prayer, depression and meditation, I realized it wasn't. Instead, God wanted to use me as an example of being steadfast and patient in a difficult situation like this, that many other women may also have to go through.

Michelle: Lakisha, like all women who have experienced a restored marriage, stopped focusing on her husband and his faults and submitted herself to God so that He could do the changing and refining that needed to be done in her. Take notice that Lakisha didn't "run" from her problems but instead she chose to "embrace" them and took hold of God's promise and believed that "NOTHING IS IMPOSSIBLE WITH GOD." Lakisha realized and trusted that God was taking her through what the world would call a "hopeless" situation so that her testimony would be a blessing for others that would come after her.

The Lord showed me that He had to break me down to use me. I had to know the hurt to help others to heal. It also helped me appreciate my husband and my marriage!

Ministry Note: Lakisha's brokenness was the very thing that God used to bring wholeness to her life again. Just like the Psalmist says, "My sacrifice, O God, is a broken spirit; a broken and contrite heart you, God, will not despise." Ps. 51:17 (NIV)

The turning point came as I stayed in my Bible. It encouraged me to keep up the fight and I started to die to self and let God take care of everything.

It was extremely hard and heart wrenching at times, but once I began to seek the Lord and put Him first (at all times)— the man who treated me so badly became the man I needed. God changed him and he became so patient and loving and began to become the leader and a blessing to his family.

Ministry Note: By putting God first in everything, Lakisha said that her husband became the godly man she needed him to be. Again Lakisha trusted God and His word, "For the unbelieving husband has been sanctified through his wife..." 1 Corinthians 7:14 (NIV)

The Lord not only found me fit to be the mother for my stepdaughter (who we gained custody of), but I got pregnant again with our last child weeks after we found out about my new step-daughter.

During this journey, I realized that no matter who or what, God's Word is what matters and we each need to fight the good fight to be the example of God's love, mercy, grace, and forgiveness.

~ Lakisha in Washington, D.C.

Chapter 21

Maria

"It was good for me to be afflicted
so that I might learn your decrees."
—Ps. 199:71 (NIV)

"The Changes God is Making"

My marriage was restored! I know I should be writing a testimony right now (in fact months ago, because it was restored in February), but first I want to share with you this PR I wrote last year but didn't send because I knew God wanted me to wait. Before I go on, please let me ask for forgiveness; I want you, my friends, and God to forgive me because this PR was written so late. Please, Erin, forgive me and thanks for everything you and these wonderful ladies have been sharing with me. Thanks God!!!

So, the PR I wrote on September 2013 was: "I want to give God all the glory and praise His name always! He is so faithful and is a lovely God!" "It was good for me to be afflicted so that I might learn Your decrees." Psalm 119:71 (NIV). I thought last year was the worst in my life, but after finding RMI God showed me that He was using my tribulation to draw me closer to Him and teach me His word.

I was so wrong about my life. I was not the wife God created me to be.

I was contentious, I did not submit myself to my husband, parents and boss, I was not discrete and talked too much, I was not kind and gentle and I thought I was smart and beautiful enough to be envied and desired. And, I think the worst sin I committed was that God was not my First Love.

My husband was my first love and my idol. "Yet I hold this against you: You have forsaken the love you had at first." Revelation 2:4 (NIV). But when I began reading all the books from RMI and the Bible and watched the "Be Encouraged" videos, God began His great work in my life. He's been renewing my mind and changing me every day. I could see my sins and my dirty heart. I could repent everything and ask for forgiveness to my husband. And now I'm gentle and respect everybody at work. I honor my parents and try to be submissive to my husband and my boss. I know there is some work to be done in me yet, but He did great changes in me and I'm so thankful and happy. I'm not anxious anymore nor judging others.

I've been learning so much with RMI and God's word!! The principles that I learned and will be always fixed on my heart are:

1. I don't need to be anxious about tomorrow and that He will give me everything I need,

2. The Lord is my Husband so I don't need to be afraid or ashamed anymore,

3. God directs men's heart whenever He wants,

4. Don't lean on my own understanding,

5. Let go of everything and let God work,

6. I live by faith and not by signs,

7. This is a war against the enemy and not against my husband.

When I began to live these principles and many other's God put in my heart, He kindly began to change my situation. First my husband forgave me and did not hate me anymore; second he became my friend again and became kind and gentle; and then He gave me peace and love to go on this journey, trusting He controls everything and He works everything to be good.

One more important change He made was to make me love Him so much that He became my FIRST LOVE. And I'm so happy now because I could really understand that this journey is the most important journey in my life because He drew me closer to Him and prepared me to comfort others with the same love He comforts me. It made me free when I realized that everything I was living was for the purpose to help others. Praise The Lord!!

For many times during this journey, God directed my husband's heart to me. But it was only when I really understood this verse that everything really changed: "Therefore this is what the Lord says: "If you repent, I will restore you that you may serve Me; if you utter worthy, not worthless words, you will be My spokesman. Let this people turn to you, but you must not turn to them." Jeremiah 15:19. It was hard to live this principle. I had to repent and ask for God help me many times. And He helped me all the time!

I learned to pray and fast fervently and to declare the victory, giving Him the praise and the glory for even the things He was still working on. For example, one night my husband, who was living in USA, sent me a message telling me every time he spoke to me he felt the desire to ask me for forgiveness and he didn't know what he was doing anymore. I began praising My Lord and Savior thanking Him for the changes He was working on my husband. And then I began to read Ezekiel 34:11-16, thanking God because He was rescuing my husband and soon he would be back to our home.

I'm SURE SOON I will share with you my RESTORED MARRIAGE TESTIMONY. I even know the title He wants to give to my testimony: "RESTORED, Even After He Moved to Another Country."

And I hope it will encourage you to go on, trusting Him and giving Him everything. Praise Him always!

Thanks and blessings!

~ *Maria in Brazil*

Chapter 22

Charity

"For the eyes of the Lord move to and fro throughout the
earth that He may strongly support those
whose heart is completely His.
You have acted foolishly in this.
Indeed, from now on you will surely have wars."
—2 Chronicles 16:9

"Opening My Heart"

I have spent the last couple of weeks praying for direction as to how to write this Praise Report, but the words did not come as easily as I would have hoped. Below is a brief portion of my journey. I hope it is a source of encouragement to the other women who are weary in their journey, or believe their situation is hopeless.

In was long ago, in September of 2006, when I found to RMIEW upon learning my former husband was involved with his co-worker and chose to leave our family to start a new life with her. To say I was caught completely off guard would be an understatement because I, like so many others, thought I had the "perfect marriage."

It was only after being left, broken, and confused that I was asked to read the, How God Can and Will Restore Your Marriage Book.

My life has never been the same, and for the first time ever, I begin to understand the living hell I put my family through. As a young girl I was raised to be strong, take charge, speak my mind, and not take anything off a man, but the piles of rubble now called my life had taught me that kind of behavior gets you no-where in a marriage.

For five months after my former husband left, I dedicated my time to reading some of the additional resources published by Restore Ministries International, including A Wise Woman and Workers@Home. God started to work in my life, and as I was enlightened to the laws of marriage, and how God really wanted me to behave. Instead of showering my children with unlimited gifts as an expression of my love, the Lord showed me how to properly train and discipline to truly express my love towards them. Most importantly, He taught me how to really love my husband and honor him (even while he lived away from us). For the first time in my life and marriage, I really wanted to honor the man in my life the way the Lord wanted me to. It felt so right inside.

In February 2007 after having very little contact with my former husband, he called one day out of the blue to let me know he was pushing through with our divorce and needed to come by to retrieve documents such as our tax returns, etc. I was completely devastated. At the time I did not know the "Facing Divorce" book existed, and instead of moving forward in my journey, I begin to pursue my former husband and begging him to NOT divorce me. It was one of the biggest mistakes of my life as it only pushed him into quickly divorcing me, and immediately marrying the other woman in an effort to show me he was moving on.

After my former husband married the OW, I fell into a depressed state and really begin to cry out to God to help me to get out of the mess called my life.

I felt betrayed, lost, confused, and angry with God and the world. My hope was for God to restore my marriage, and put my family back together again; things were not supposed to be this way. On top of coming to terms with my former husband's recent marriage, I was dealing with poor health (due to the "infidelity diet", I had lost 30% of my body weight), foreclosure, work-related issues, and my grandmother still working with my former husband and reporting back all the workplace rumors to me, even as I tried to find peace.

Ladies, but how many of us know that when life looks like it is at its worse, Jesus is at His best.

The day I received my divorce decree I remember praying and asking God to give me the wisdom to raise my children so that they would not become statistics of divorce or being a part of a single-parent family. My mother has chosen to divorce my father when I was 12-years old and not to long afterwards, I ended up pregnant with my first child at 15. In addition to my parents' divorce, my grandparents, and also my former husband's mother and grandmother also experienced multiple marriages and divorces. This was not the heritage I wanted to leave for my children. With all of this in mind, my children's future, and knowing my vulnerable condition, I chose to resign from my position with our telecommunications company, and dedicate my life to being a stay at home mother and worker at home. It was at this time, the Lord led me to homeschool my children. My life has never been the same.

I wish I could report that this was the end of my trials and tribulations on my way to a restored marriage and family, but sadly it is not. Since my former husband was now married to the OW and had gone on to have two children with her, I felt like God was telling me to move on with my life. I severed my relationship with this ministry and chose to move on with my life in hope of finally close the book on this horrible nightmare.

To my detriment, I continued to remain in contact with my former mother in law, begin to confide in family and friends, and completely treated my former husband as a social outcast in an effort to "protect myself and my children" from anymore pain. This led him to breaking his relationship with me and constantly skipping out on the children when it was time for them to visit him. By God's grace, he continued to support us financially which lessen the blow to our devastating condition.

Things begin to improve in our lives in the fall of 2009 when I was able to get a job working from home and we finally got our own apartment. This was after living with my family for almost two and a half years. I had spent enough time in the desert of despair, homelessness, unemployment, and anger.

The kids and I were happy; and our lives were good. The Lord had brought different home schooling friends into my life and everything was finally coming together. Because of his rich mercy, God started to deal with me about the unforgiveness I still had in my heart towards my former husband. After such a long time, I thought everything was fine because we could talk long enough to exchange the kids, but that was it and God required more. To prove that he was moving me into the direction of forgiveness, my former husband started reaching out to me and wanted to become more involved with our kids.

For so long the kids had been only mine, and now he wanted to come back. I did not agree with his request inwardly, and outwardly I did not welcome his efforts. You see, in addition to mending his relationship with our kids, my former husband was making an effort to mend his friendship with me, at the time I was unable to get past my own hurts the see what he needed the most from me. My forgiveness. My former husband wanted to start making mutual decisions concerning our kids, and to reclaim his role in their lives, but I was not quick to let go, finally after continually brushing him off he tired of the tug of war with me and I was served with custody paper on December 22, 2010. I officially lost custody of my children December 31, 2010. It was the darkest moment of my life.

To make a long story short, experiencing divorce was nothing compared to the loss of my children. It was at this moment that I realized the one person I was offended by the most, was the person who now had control of what I loved more than anything, my children. I knew only God could help me. My former husband still wanted a friendship, I wanted recompense, and the Lord wanted restoration. I prayed continually for God to soften my heart and help me to heal.

Even though I had been baptized many years ago, I believe this was when I became a real Christian. In learning about the grace of God and His love towards us, I was able to finally forgive my former husband and the other woman from my heart. I had tried to forgive many times before and did, but this time I was able to walk in the freedom of Christ without fear. Once healed, it no longer matter to me that he was married to her, I was healed and Jesus had made me whole.

While I was not running into situations to see them together, God has taught me how to deal with our interactions with a meek and humble spirit.

Finally, in the summer of 2011, my former husband asked me to please forgive him for leaving me and admit to the mistake he had made. I never thought I would hear these words, but I was thankful to God that I did.

After His confession, the Lord brought the ladies of RMIEW back into my life to protect me from making further mistakes in my restoration journey. After my former husband's confession, I was tempted in my heart to pursue him if for nothing else his friendship, but I learned in the RRR not to make this fatal mistake.

Also I pulled out of attending church, completely cut off my relationship with my former mother in law, and begin to open my heart to God's will for my life, which is the same as it has always been, to restore my marriage, and now my relationship to my children by restoring my custody.

You see, even though my former husband married the other woman and had children with her, God's plan for my life has not changed. I simply got off the path or the narrow road as we have learned it is really called. A few months ago I was completely adamant about NOT being restored to my former husband, but God (who is so rich in mercy) has allowed me to see the pain my children would continue to experience if I did not open my heart to His will.

As the adult child of divorce parents, it is one of the greatest burdens of my life as feeling torn during birthdays, holidays, graduations, etc. By opening myself to God's will for my life, I finally have peace, no matter what He decides. Who knows what the future holds for me?

It was only in opening my heart to restoration of my family, that I was able to receive the blessing when my former husband insisted that I take our children for the entire summer. I am only "allowed" 30 days usually. This is the longest time I have possessed my children since losing custody of them. I am so thankful.

Also since my son had a hard time in school this year, and did not pass our state's standardized testing, I have the chance to home school my son over the break. It has been a desire for my kids to return to home school since they left. His terrible school year, led their father to sending them to me and the Lord has placed many things on my heart in order to help the kids over the summer. God has told me all year, "Do not despise the day of small beginnings," and my heart is resting in this promise.

While the restoration of my entire family is still a way off, I am so happy at what God is doing in my life right now. Things are still rocky, but progress is steady. What more could I ask for?

~ *Charity in Oklahoma*

Chapter 23

Liana

"Your adversary, the devil,
Prowls around like a roaring lion,
Seeking someone to devour."
—1 Peter 5:8

"Left the Door Open"

Six years ago I met my FH and it was like my destiny. We knew we belonged together and the bond grew stronger by the day. I was an executive and he owned his own business. It wasn't much for him to exist on, but that was not even a thought. Soon, our lives began to turn upside down.

I came to RMI because I believed my EH and I were meant to be together. That God was there the day He married us and made us one flesh together with the spirit of the Lord. Unfortunately, my husband said he likes his life of independence and can not ever see himself living ever again with a woman—and not me for sure. I felt as if he had thrown it all away without asking for help from God to restore our marriage. Only I have been the person to continue to ask and He answered by sending me here, to you, to learn what I did wrong and how to change.

Even though we were both Born Again Christians with charismatic testimonies, we were about to fall. Here again, being saved doesn't mean it is over and life is like walking in sunshine.

It wasn't. The devil came against us because I left the door open to him. In every way possible this beautiful love affair faded to grey really fast. Though we did have good moments, they weren't enough to offset the bad ones when the fighting became an act of strength as to who would survive. By the way, I was never the winner in a fight. I wanted to be, but I always submitted in tears of repentance, but deep down inside was a brewing tempest. The bitterness was becoming the cornerstone of our frail marriage.

When I came here, I considered myself a Baptist. I was saved 2 months after I met my EH. We were always listening to Christian music and one weekend I came home and we had a fight and I decided it was over. Then the next day I listened to Michael W Smith Worship CD and he said..."like a rose trampled on the ground and in that moment I saw the vision of what my Lord had done for someone as rebellious as me. I cried on my carpet, face down, for 5 hours. I prayed for repentance and that I finally understood all the years of going to church, the message I had missed...I now understood. Since coming here, I love the Lord with all my heart and believe He has been with me through this marriage trial from start to completion.

When I came here, in my Marriage Evaluation Questionnaire, I said, "I believe in the will of God and I also believe in marriage. I never did believe in divorce. My husband has not been faithful to me. He does not appear to be a saved Christian any longer and has some beliefs that are outside of the bible. I believe the enemy has crushed our marriage. My entire family has fought against us and done some excruciating things to both of us a s a couple. No one has really come alongside us to support it. My EH has had troubles for years making money and was somewhat living under what was my roof when we met.

I thought the pressure of having somewhere to live would be off him but instead it created terrible insecurities. I feel that his family told him how unstable it all was here with me.

Unfortunately, he never did commit to the marriage from the start. I'm afraid, I suppose, that my marriage is going to end in divorce because my EH was sleeping with a secular woman and is somehow mesmerized by her. He was pushing me to end our and I was offering him reconciliation at every turn until I finally gave in feeling it must be God's will to end something that never had a chance to work.

Quite honestly, my EH is very controlling and punishes me constantly. He finds my weaknesses and attacks in hard via emails he sends to me. It has been really rough without him and by his retaliation. I almost succeeded in starving myself to death and succeeded in losing 40 pounds. My hair has fallen out entirely and my health is only borderline. I still cannot believe he is not in bed with me when I wake in the morning. I have constant nightmares about this situation. I feel I not only lost a husband but also am so worried because he has backslid in the secular world due to this OW. Tell me, do we even have a chance? The divorce was signed by the judge a week after receipt even though this was supposed to take a couple of months. I thought I would adjust but I haven't. Can you help me? Nothing is getting better and I am not moving on as I believe I should. Do I have any reason to believe we can find our happiness we had the day we first met?

So, my former husband had left me over and over again. It was heartbreaking. I was crying inside and deeply wounded. I would beg him to return home to me each time and after a few days of calm, he would come home, saying we would work it out. Each time I became more insecure until it came to a final break. I knew we were in serious trouble. I was fine for a few days when at first he left and then I began to feel very uncomfortable. The first email he sent was to tell me that this separation was indefinite and the next email was that he had found another woman.

I couldn't even be jealous or angry. He simply went to someone who could give him the life he wanted. One of calm. Our families fought against our marriage and admittedly we went to our respective families to spill out our problems.

This was the worst error of all. If we only knew the damage it created. To this day my family is not speaking to me so when I came to RMI, I was totally alone.

Prior to RMI I sought help through pastors, Christian counseling and traditional therapy. None of it worked. In fact, it made everything so much worse. They all said it was hopeless and gone beyond repair. I was so disappointed. I cried like a baby every day. I was totally unable to move and didn't eat. I lost 45 pounds and at my age of 61, it left me with some wrinkles that were not there before and a lot of hair loss. I know a lot of women mourn the marriage like I did. It went on for months like that.

No matter what answers I was looking for scripturally, no one was willing to look them up for me or explain the scriptures that I found. Basically the demons were pulling me in one direction and God was pulling me in another.

In my loneliness I called my ex-fiancé from over 20 years before. We had always remained friends and I guess I needed someone desperately to speak to. Instead what I got was a secular view of of how the world sees my situation and he too worked on me to believe divorce was the way to go and so I filed for divorce after a lot of meditation. My FH also wanted me to file and get it done. His life had moved on according to him. In my haste and wanting to take things slower, I left it to God and filed the first set of divorce papers myself in tears.

The second set was different. I had already found RMI and knew that I had to proceed in obedience to my husband. In an unbelievable emotionless state, I filed. The court told me it would take up to 3 months to complete, but in only a week it was granted and immediately I fell on the floor face down and cried out to the Lord.

After reading the first chapters of Erin's book on divorce it is critical for all women who are faced with Divorce to read just the first 2 chapters. I immediately came to an understanding of what was going on and began to live the life Jesus would want me to.

I came to place of contentment and peace. I understood why God would want this from me and how obedience was the key, so I began to follow it to the letter of how Erin walked me through this process in her book. My life would never be the same: Our problem was never an issue of love, it was intense and always there. My problem was control and staying in control.

When I realized I tore my own house down, I sat down with the Lord and cried out for His help and to never leave me. I knew I had to be broken. I can't recall how many times I asked to be broken, but it was a number of times. It truly felt like the fresh fires each time. Days would go by where I stayed to myself and prayed in my prayer closet privately to the Lord. I knew if things were going to change that God was going to do the changing. I released my will over to Him and allowed Him to be the boss of me. As I prayed in praise and a change for my heart, I prayed also for my husband to turn his heart towards me.

For those people who are walking dead in the world, not knowing there is a living God who seeks out the broken and wants to show you a life of prosperity in many ways, they are sadly missing what I have found myself. My time in the prayer closet was invaluable. As I look at houses to replace my condo, one thing is certain, I must have that space where only the Lord and I can continue our relationship of deep spiritual love.

Today I have more than a hope and future and see His plan. I still have to work at precepts and concepts of God's laws on a regular basis and the work of changing me will continue. I literally poured myself out over the past few months: Seeing my past, realizing I could not live that way any longer. It is a very narrow road and certainly not one for the faint of heart. Refining yourself to the image God has of you is the goal.

The Lord taught me to put all of my faith in Him alone. That I can work with Him to His glory by simply reading my Bible and praying according to His word. That fighting in the flesh is a useless exercise. That can be applied not just in marriages, but in all situations and relationships.

Knowing that by our faith in God we can fight in the spirit and the mind alone without a word spoken to any other person was the greatest lesson of all. God helped me to see my past hurts. He walked me through each one of them. My adoption as a child, and my family's rejection has been the worst one of all. Then I realized that Abba was really my Father and that I can go to Him with my deep scars to be healed.

Looking back at a past full of pain is very difficult and yet it is the very thing that forms who we are. That there is a world out there who has little time for someone in pain is an area where I hope I can help others win the battle.

It really is the enemy and his co-workers who keep you stuck in those moments of heart pain. We can control that by going to God and asking Him to reveal the secrets of our pain one by one and He will faithfully process it all as we look to Him.

God is amazing. He never gave me too much at one time, and yet it was painful, but He healed the wounds. How great is our God? It was then that I was able to see the wife that I was to be to my husband, the mother to my children and the sister to my brothers. It all had to change.

The turning point was finally letting it all go and allowing my former husband to have his experience. I have always held on literally to him when he tried to leave me. I must have let go a half a dozen times during our separation and many times when I stumbled, I received a nasty letter back. I praised the Lord even in those moments because in it I learned that praise was what was necessary to win this war, not pursuing someone who has left us. And also, to tighten up my mouth. God knew it was a weakness and set me apart from everyone until I learned that vital lesson.

My restoration began to happen one day that I was praying in my closet and mentioned to the Lord that I hadn't heard from my husband in 3 weeks and that it would be nice to receive a line of email from him. The next day he wrote a line to me.

I wrote back and mentioned I was going up to a Bible camp north of here. He said in an impulse that that would make a nice trip and would I like him to go with me. I said yes of course and we had a lovely drive and talked, though I mostly listening to how badly his relationships with women and family had been. I stayed rather quiet and listened. Some of it was hurtful.

That day we made it to a powerful spirit filled service at the camp and one at night. We had gone for a swim in the lake and the day was perfect. That night he admitted he didn't know how this happened but God had given him insight into the work I had done just to win him back and that no one else would love him that deeply to do that. Later he said it was true what I had prayed that God gave him back 7 times the love we had when we first met. It is all so supernatural.

This Restoration Journey is the only way back to have a restored life. It is imperative that we follow the books and videos offered by this ministry—without missing a step in any of it. To read and re-read everything is vital. Taking the time and committing it to the Lord is why. I can only have gratitude in my heart for showing me the way RMI. I was lost and now am found. I recommend this to ministry everyone... Christian or not.

Today, because of what I have gone through, I am absolutely sold out to helping other women who are in marriage crisis.

In conclusion, you can fall down and get back up again and the Lord is still willing to help you. He is the finest Counselor in the world and there is no need to go elsewhere. If you have been damaged by your church or therapy as I was, it can all be mended by going through this journey that is set out in these courses and books. There is something greater than us....God!

Just to speak His name and He is there every time. Do you know anyone like that? I don't! He changed my person and my life.

~ *Liana in Australia*

Atarah

"Honor your father and your mother,
that your days may be long upon the land
which the Lord your God is giving you."
—Exodus 20:12 NJKV

"RESTORED to Parents"

I have been a Christian for 10 years and at the beginning of my faith journey, I was passionate and on fire. My parents (who are Muslim) found out about my new faith and asked me to leave the home. Looking back now, I can see that's where a foothold had been given to the devourer. I became angry and conceited, and wore several masks to avoid feeling rejected or hurt again.

Soon after I married my husband, who was used to my angry and verbally aggressive outbursts. During our 7-year marriage, he left the marital home twice and in October 2013 he left for what he says 'the last time'. During the 7 years I barely spoke to my parents and would often reject them. I felt further rejected by them when I told them I was getting married to a Christian man and they told me I was never welcome at home again. I lost trust in my parents, in fact all parents, even my husband's. I could often be heard saying "you can't trust parents", "their love is conditional", etc. I also lost all respect for parents and convinced myself that they didn't deserve love or understanding.

When my husband left me, I finally found the courage to go round to my parents' house. They were so happy to see me. I felt the Lord tell me that their love has always been there, and that I had held onto my hurt and had been rejecting them for the last few years.

When my wedding anniversary and New Year's Day came, I stayed round their house for a long weekend and when I left my father said to me "there is always a bed here for you". This touched my heart more than anything else as I finally felt that I had my parents back. I realized that I have been the prodigal daughter here, and my parents love for me is an expression of my Heavenly Father's love for me. I also noted my parents' response to me coming home (no expectations, just love) and know that's what God has called me to be like when my earthly husband comes home.

I thank God that He is a God of restoration. He has restored my relationship with my parents which I thought would never happen. I thought I would always be an 'orphan' and during the darkest days of my life in the last 3 months, God saw fit to turn the children's heart back towards the parents, and the parents heart towards their child. I feel blessed by His goodness to me and the fire in my heart is once again also being reignited for the Lord and His Word.

Healed from the Fear of Silence

My husband left the marriage in October 2013, and I know you will all understand when I say how difficult the journey is on the narrow road that we have chosen. We have no children so I found myself left in the house. Though I work in Christian Ministry and have a big family, the loneliness that pervades one's inner soul when the one you love leaves- is potentially paralysing. The worst days were Sundays as that's the day you would see couples together in town or taking walks.

From the onset after he left- I spent as much time as I could with other people. And if I wasn't with other people then I would be on the phone calling others so I wouldn't have to sit with myself. Slowly God started to work in my heart.... I saw the 'hate wall' come down between my husband and I, and then go back up again. That was mid-January and the communication lines hadn't reopened. So I have had to learn to live with silence a lot over the last four months, and this has been so uncomfortable. Coming from a family of 7 children and both my parents- quietness isn't something we were used to. Even when I prayed to the Lord I would fill the silence with words rather than be able to sit back and listen to Him speak to me.

This all came to a head on Wednesday when I realised that the silence I was in was deafening. I hadn't heard from my EH, I lived alone and no-one understood. As I spoke to a friend they asked me about silence and I explained that silence was a common weapon used between my parents when we were younger particularly when they had conflict. As the more extrovert child I would try and break through my parents silence through humour as it was so uncomfortable and I never knew what would happen to my parents if they continued not talking to each other. My friend and I prayed and God invaded. He showed me the root of my fear of silence, and the ways the enemy has used that in my marriage as my EH is a 'silent type'. I realised that though we weren't living together at present, his silence had bought the same feelings of fear and powerlessness. **God delivered me!!!** It was instantaneous and immediately I felt a peace come over me. Since then I have been able to sit more with myself, listen to the Lord and hear Him speak to me. I have felt less afraid and more close to the Lord as my Heavenly Husband.

This season of my life is bringing to the surface all the debris the Lord wants to deal with, and I am so blessed and grateful that He would do that, bring me here to learn more about Him and to heal. I now feel like a woman, rather than a little girl. Though this season was painful, I know that the birth pains are signs that God is changing me into the woman He wants me to be—a woman of dignity, with a boldness for the Lord. So stay strong ladies, as God wants this season with you on your own... to be the woman and wife my HH has always desired me to be. Dear friend, He is working on your behalf in your situation, trust Him alone to do that and allow Him to spend this time perfecting and loving you.

~Atarah in the United Kingdom

——————————Chapter 25——————————

Raeesa

"The steadfast love of the Lord never ceases;
his mercies never come to an end;
they are new every morning;
great is your faithfulness."
—Lamentations 3:22-23 ESV

"RESTORED in England"

After 4 years together and 2 children my husband and I were finally married. Then just 10 weeks later he announced he didn't love me anymore and he was leaving.

In just a few weeks he changed completely, so much so, that I didn't recognize him. He soon became involved with a woman at work and we barely spoke other than arrangements for our children.

This is when I began to seek the Lord, after my husband left— I was desperate and alone. Slowly I became stronger and began to watch Erin's Be Encouraged videos and absorbed all her wisdom. After watching them over and over, I was no longer angry or bitter and instead I used my time and energy to pray every day for my husband's safe return and salvation.

The principles the Lord taught me during this trial was that without Him, life is pointless. He needs to be the centre and focus of our existence and no matter how we are hurting He can always heal our pain and deliver us from the enemy IF we stay close by Him and trust in His direction. Sometimes it seems you're going off course, like letting go, but if you stay connected to Him, He will carefully guide you.

The most difficult times that God helped me through were the many times I was so low, so close to the point of giving in to what the world says to do or how I felt. I begged the Lord often to take me away and stop the misery I was living in. At one point I didn't care about anyone or anything anymore.

That's when I came to the "turning point" of my restoration. As my focus began to turn solely on the Lord and nothing else (as Erin and this ministry tells us to do but few do) my husband started to come by more and called often. Instead of getting too excited, I remained friendly and didn't reject his interest—but remained focused on the Lord. Throughout my trials the Lord told me to hang on for 6 months and to trust Him. That date came and went, but He still remained with me.

Please understand that many times things seem to get worse the closer I got. I would get word of him and the other woman and so very nearly gave up, but each time the Lord delivered me. My husband came by one evening 6 months to the day he left just like the Lord promised and suggested that we could try to work things out. However, that's when things got really difficult, since he remained very clinical for a while. But I remained calm and did not challenge his requests. Then just 3 short weeks later, he returned home. He has since cut off contact with the other woman and to help stay true, changed jobs. Although our marriage still has a long way to go to fully be what God designed, I am confident that we will only become stronger.

I would highly recommend staying steadfast and true to the Lord and also Erin's literature. If not, I would not be where I am today. When I asked my husband what brought him home he answered that I had changed, something about me drew him home and he couldn't explain what it was.

You see it was the Lord within me that drew my husband to my side. Also, without my acceptance of His love and allowing the healing that needed to take place, this would never have been possible.

Now I am very interested in helping encourage other women. Let me begin by saying to each of you:

Please please never give up no matter how the enemy taunts you or hurts you. Instead keep your focus on where you need to be with your focus on the Lord and the truth of the literature from this ministry.

~ Raeesa in England RESTORED

Chapter 26

Rita

"Give to everyone who asks you,
and if anyone takes what belongs to you,
do not demand it back.
Do to others as you would have them do to you."
—Luke 6:30-31

"Restored Twice"

My initial journey began when I was led to RMI in July 2004. My husband and I had been married for 20 years. I was his third wife. I was separated from my husband with two small kids who cried for him everyday. I was desperate to find a solution to put my marriage back together. I grew up in the church but was given a lot of bad advice; advice that went against God's Word and what He commands us to do. While at work I typed in the words "marriage restoration" and was led to Restore Ministries International. I read Erin's testimony and thought it was the most incredible thing I'd ever heard. No one, not in my church, my family or any friend had ever given me the hope I received from RMI. I knew then that God would restore my marriage and He was the answer I had been looking for.

My husband and I were separated for two and a half years. During that time, I devoured the How God Can and Will Restore Your Marriage (often known as RYM), A Wise Woman, and the Workers at Home books.

I couldn't get enough of God's truths that were contained within their pages. The more I read, the more broken I felt and the more I knew that unless I submitted my life to the Lord, things in my marriage and my life would never change. I was in so much emotional pain that I knew God would have to completely heal me.

Although God did heal me of my pain, I was only willing to let Him heal me partially. I only did what I needed to do to bring my husband home. The Lord was not my primary focus, and I didn't consider Him as my Husband. I fooled myself into believing that God had changed me completely but He wasn't through with me yet.

After God restored my marriage to my husband, I was ecstatic and once again the Lord was not first in my life. I put off helping others, as God wanted me to do, and once again fell into that ditch of contention. The old destructive anger and spiritual arrogance resurfaced. I wasn't walking in God's forgiveness or His amazing love and I found it almost impossible to forgive. This went on for years. However, God in His love and grace for me showed me mercy and blessed me (and my husband) with two restoration babies, which I prayed for during our separation. My husband said that he felt unloved, and I didn't trust him with my feelings or to make any of the financial or other decisions for our family. Eventually the inevitable happened. I tore down my house and once again God removed my husband from me.

This time, I just knew that God would not restore my marriage. I was so angry and "fed up" that I didn't want Him to restore it. We were separated numerous times prior to this one and both had committed adultery during our marriage. I even stopped wearing my wedding ring when I found out about the OW. I felt extremely hurt, angry, discouraged, humiliated, and rejected all over again. I didn't want the constant reminder, through my wedding band, of my pains and failures, nor did I want to be physically attached to my husband.

I began to believe what others were telling me about my marriage —
there was no hope, my earthly husband   would never change, and I
should just divorce him, move on and find someone else. I was
completely double-minded.

I would have days when I wanted my marriage restored and days when
I didn't. Whenever I considered divorce, God would bring me back to
His Word and confirm to me that He hates divorce and doesn't want
this for me. I wasn't sure what I wanted, but I did remember the peace
and love I felt when I'd gotten closer to the Lord the first time on my
journey. I wanted that feeling back.

My two older children were full of anger over the separation and the
two younger ones were confused. Neither my family nor my in-laws
wanted us to remain married. In fact, my in-laws remained friends with
my husband's second wife.

However, I wanted God's best for our family and victory over
everything the enemy was trying to do to destroy us. I lost hope that
my marriage would be restored again especially since I received the
truth twice and still messed up. Through the teeter tottering of my
emotions, God kept bringing the RYM book and Wise Woman books,
and it's principles to the surface of my mind. I knew I wasn't the wife
God called me to be. I learned the principles detailed in these books but
stopped applying them. He kept pursuing me about them and I gave in,
thinking that perhaps I should re-read them and re-join RMI. I obeyed
God and rejoined RMI.

It was one of the best things that ever happened to me. I learned what
my role as a wife and mother was, and that God was to be first in my
life in everything I do. I felt such conviction when the truth was
revealed to me. It started such a desire to live a life pleasing to God. I
finally found the truth that I'd been looking for but couldn't find, not
even in my own home church.

I enrolled in the courses offered through RMI and began studying God's Word regularly and read the Encouragers and Praise Reports daily. This helped to re-establish hope in my heart. I promised the Lord that I would let Him restore, rebuild, and renew my life. Unlike the first time, this time around I found my First Love, surrendered my all to Him, and discovered that narrow path that leads to the abundant life God has for me!

He taught me that no one is ever going to love me more than He does, and that He does not like when I place other people or things first in my heart where only He belongs. He reminded me the importance of forgiveness and how to watch what I say to those who have authority in my life, especially my earthly husband   .

God showed me how to be His bride and have a gentle and quiet spirit, which is precious to Him. He taught me how to love those who are unlovable and unforgivable. He led me to be nonjudgmental and understanding of others so I may have healthy relationships and not put myself in a position to be abandoned or abused.

God taught me how to be an encouraging woman; a minister of reconciliation to other hurting ladies and the Titus woman that Erin and so many others who send in encouragement have been to me. The Lord showed me how to be obedient through my sufferings. He taught me how to take every concern and every aspect of my life to Him and to trust only Him with my life - both on earth and in eternity. Through my tough times, God prodded me to submit blindly by getting out of the boat like Peter and keeping my eyes centered on Jesus, the Author and Finisher of my faith. The Lord taught me how to enjoy every day of my journey with Him. He showed me that He is never going to leave me or forsake me. God taught me so many wonderful things that I did not know.

Those wonderful things the Lord showed me were not easy to learn. I had to constantly die to self and press into the Lord closer so He could increase His presence in my life.

There were times where I had to show love and respect to those people who were out to emotionally and spiritually harm me. The Lord showed me how to turn the other cheek. "But I [Jesus] say this to you who are listening: Love your enemies, do good to those who hate you, bless those who curse you, pray for those who treat you badly.

To anyone who slaps you on one cheek, present the other cheek as well; to anyone who takes your cloak from you, do not refuse your tunic. Give to everyone who asks you, and do not ask for your property back from someone who takes it. "Treat others as you would like people to treat you..." You will have a great reward, and you will be children of the Most High for He Himself is kind to the ungrateful and the wicked." (Luke 6:27-31,35) For the first time in my life, He became my all and everything and I was no longer concerned with earthly matters, including my marriage. I was content to live a life of "singleness", as Erin and so many women in this ministry have expressed, with my Wonderful Husband.

I did not give my marriage or the affairs of my husband any thought. I kept my focus on the Lord and His promises to me. My earthly husband would tell me (or our children) that he was coming home but it no longer mattered. I continued to encourage others. I had, and still do, such a deep desire to live a life that not only pleases the Lord but also a desire to help other hurting women to put their faith and trust in The Lord.

I wanted, for a few years now, to be more fruitful in my life. I was genuinely delighted hearing or reading restoration testimonies for other women. When my focus was completely off of my marriage and I was content in my circumstances, the Lord blessed me with a restored marriage.

My encouragement to you is to really seek the Lord. Give Him your whole heart in every area of your life. Don't hold anything back. It may be painful but only for a season. On the other side of pain is healing and restoration.

I highly recommend ALL the resources that this ministry offers — the books, videos, daily Encouragers, the courses — everything! Each resource helped me to renew my mind, restore me back to my First Love, and to rebuild my life on the solid foundation of God's Word. Don't resist following any of the principles, such as letting go of your church. It was being absent from the church where I enriched my relationship with the Lord.

I am eternally grateful for this ministry, Erin, all the Ministers and Ministers in Training who opened up their lives and encouraged me to keep pressing into the Lord and to not give up. It amazes me when I think of it or talk about it but I wouldn't change one thing that has happened on my Restoration Journey!

It is my heart's desire for God to use me to help other hurting women, including my daughters, building their lives on the sinking sand of the world's lies about their roles of being a wife, mother and child of the King. I don't want to just go to "church" and not have a more intimate relationship with God. I want to be able to lead my daughters and other women by word and deed, to desire to be all that God created us to be. God placed a desire in my heart to be a Godly wife and to honor my husband and be the helper suitable that He intended for me to be. I won't let Satan win and take my focus off of what really matters—Him!

Don't let the enemy destroy you or your family thus leaving a life's legacy riddled with sin to your children and future generations. God has an incredible love for you that you can't even fathom. He is such an awesome God and has such wonderful plans for us. He wants and deserves to be First in our hearts and in our lives—being loved by His Son.

The Lord wants and deserves to be First in our hearts and in our lives. We've given that position to our spouses, or children or jobs, and none of them has satisfied us. I encourage you to give the Lord your heart and hold nothing back. The life He has for you will blow your mind!

~ *Rita in Texas*

Chapter 27

Shorts

"Was no one found who returned
to give glory to God,
except one?"
—Luke 17:18

"Restored Awhile Ago"

Hi There!! I just wanted to let everyone there know my marriage is restored. It wasn't restored the way I ever thought it would be, but PRAISE GOD, we are restored and what's even better—my relationship with the LORD is stronger than I ever dreamed it could or would be.

My marriage was restored a while ago, but I just wasn't sure how to contact the ministry, I'm hoping someone gets this message now. Would you like me to type up a testimony to share?

~ *Lisa in Texas*

Ministry Note: We wrote back "Yes" but never got a full testimony. Sometimes He works so fast that we are in awe:

"Pleasant and Loving Spouse"

Hello, I'm sorry for the follow-up email (I know that you discourage it) but wonderful things happened just hours after taking your questionnaire. Encouraging Women advised me not to call him, so I got off the phone with him when he called, and told him to have a nice day and while doing your first week of lessons, we were restored.

~ Jill in Arizona

Within Hours my Miracle Came!

After 2 1/2 years of mostly living separate, I came home to a renewed spouse that had dinner waiting for me and a lot of love. Not only was my husband there asking to come home, he was now pleasant and loving. He told me that someone at his job (a pastor) that he'd never spoken to besides saying hello and goodbye, told him that his family needs and loves him and that he needed to seek salvation, turn to the Lord, and most of all...Go home! Needless to say God speaks through you and I can't thank you enough for all the support and advice from encouragingwomen.org.

~ April in Florida

Ministry Note: Only ONE in 10 that we help will come back to give God glory. Over the 25 years in ministry, I've found that this appears to be fairly accurate when women and especially men show up YEARS later saying they've been restored for years but never told us.

So to make sure you are able to give God the praise for restoring 10 times what we share in our Encouragers, I just uncovered two more RESTORED marriages today that I stumbled on—women who have built their own websites and wrote books—without ever contacting me or RMI—to let us know their marriages had been restored and that they had gone on to have their own ministries :)

"Blessed is the man who trusts in the LORD and whose trust is the LORD. For he will be like a tree planted by the water, that extends its roots by a stream and will not fear when the heat comes; but its leaves will be green, and it will not be anxious in a year of drought nor cease to yield fruit'"—Jeremiah 17:9-10

"Trust in the LORD with all your heart and do not lean on your own understanding. In all your ways acknowledge Him, and He will make your paths straight"—Proverbs 3:4-6

Remarried with God First!

I just wanted to let you know that my ex-husband and I have remarried to each other for the 5th and final time! Life is good with us and our 3 children. As long as you have God first in your life, you can and will conquer anything.

~ Jodi-Anne in Tennessee

---Chapter 28---

Busela

"Behold, I am the LORD, the God of all flesh;
is anything too difficult for Me?"
—Jeremiah 32:27

Part 1

"RESTORED in 3 Months"

I started on the journey to my restoration in September 2013. I had been looking for something that would help me grow and develop my spiritual being as well as help take my focus off my situation. The first thing I learned is that I had been contentious; secondly I learned that I had not put God as my First Love; thirdly I learned that I had build my home on sinking sand. With all this I needed to replace the bad and wrong with the right principles, there was no better place than to do that with the Lord. The lessons I have gone through have elevated my faith and trust in the Lord! I'm now at a point where I confidently say nothing is impossible with God!!!

My seemingly impossible marital situation was just a piece of cake for the Lord. My husband left me on the 15th of March 2013. On the 5th of December he called me to a meeting with his psychologist to tell me he wanted a divorce. He read a long letter of all I did to hurt him, I remained calm right through and acknowledged I was wrong. This is something I would never have done in my own strength, this can only be God.

I had to seriously fight the flesh from screaming at him and giving him my list of how he hurt me. I realized that day that God was really working in me. I applied the principles I learned through this ministry and told him I would not like to be divorced but I will not stand in his way if he wants it. I told him if that's what will make him happy, I will gladly sign the divorce papers. Not only did I just say this but I meant it.

From this day on my husband started making contact twice or more a week to check on the kids and just chit chatting. The frequency of calls increased as the days went by. In January our 2-year old started crèche and he voluntarily offered to pick her up from school everyday. This meant seeing him almost everyday as I was still on maternity leave, I tried by all means to avoid him but when I wasn't home he'd wait for me. The contact improved to regular SMSs during the day as well. On the 13th of February, he came out straight that he had changed his mind about the divorce, praise God! On the 15th of February he moved back home!

Our God is really faithful. We are working on restoration of our marriage and I'm trusting God for complete restoration.

~ *Busela in South Africa*

Ministry Note: Busela went from Facing Divorce to a Restored Marriage in just 3 Months. Below is her full testimony!

Restoration Part 2

"Run Over by Ex, NOW RESTORED"

"Crushed; perplexed, but not despairing;
persecuted, but not forsaken;
struck down, but not destroyed."
1 Corinthians 4:8-9

My seemingly impossible marital situation was just a piece of cake for the Lord. My husband left me and 3 months later he called me to a meeting with his psychologist to tell me he wanted a divorce. During the meeting he read a long letter of all I did to hurt him, but I remained calm right through and acknowledged I was wrong. This is something I would never have done in my own strength, this can only be God. I had to seriously fight the flesh from screaming at him and giving him my list of how he hurt me. I realized that day that God was really working in me. I applied the principles I learned through this ministry and told him I would not like to be divorced but I will not stand in his way if he wants it. I told him if that's what will make him happy, I will gladly sign the divorce papers. Not only did I just say this but I meant it.

From this day on my husband started making contact twice or more a week to check on the kids and just chit chatting. The frequency of calls increased as the days went by. When our 2-year old started crèche (a nursery where babies and young children are cared for during the working day) and he voluntarily offered to pick her up from school everyday. This meant seeing him almost everyday as I was still on maternity leave, I tried by all means to avoid him but when I wasn't home he'd wait for me. The contact improved to regular SMSs during the day as well. Soon he came out straight that he had changed his mind about the divorce, praise God! And 2 weeks later he moved back home!

When Busela came to us, in her questionnaire she wrote "I am a Christian, got saved in 1998.

I have experienced the hand of God upon my life. His grace and unfailing love saw me through a terrible accident when my ex-husband ran me over with a car and when I lost my first child in 2008. I have learnt to fully depend on Him. My husband says his main issues with me is that I'm clingy and demanding.

We got married in 2011, and I'm currently pregnant due in any day and have a 19-month-old daughter. We have five kids in total as my husband has 4 other kids from previous relationships. We live with two of his kids, three in total including mine.

The crux of our problems is my husband's failure to priorities our marriage above all, except God of course, and instead sacrificing our marriage for his 11-year old (who leaves with us). My husband has no boundaries when it comes to this child as a result no discipline. Secondly we have poor communication, we just don't talk, because we do things without communicating, we clash. Thirdly, my husband has no sense of commitment to our marriage, six months into our marriage he was talking divorce after we have a huge disagreement. Fourthly, he is of the view that his children do not have to respect me as I'm not their mother and this he has openly communicated to the 11-year old. Lastly, our intimacy is almost non extent.

We both had to adjust from leaving as a single into a full house and full time parenting of 3 children soon after we got married. He moved out of our home in March, ever since there has been strife and continuous disagreements.

My husband hasn't been cooperative in all counseling sessions we had with our pastors and counsellors either. I believe our issues are minor and can be easily resolved, however there doesn't seem to be willingness from his side. So I want help but my husband doesn't.

Then she began submitting one praise report after another, like this one:

When I came I was separated and I started on the RMI courses right away. Wow God is truly faithful!

Since I am on maternity leave which means, this leave has turned into a spiritual leave and I'm loving every moment of it! In the last month the holy spirit has been prompting me to go on a Facebook fast, I've been resisting for sometime now.

Well this week I decided to get on it for 7 days, one of my prayer points is for God to help me walk in my calling and to experience the glow, contentment and fulfillment spoken about in the lessons. Boy oh boy the glow is so overwhelming, everyone I come into contact with feels God's presence and they just want to stay in my presence. This can only be God!! I'm so much at peace despite my marital situation.

At this point, my husband wasn't not home yet, but he has asked me to join him to a meeting with his psychologist to bring closure to our situation. I didn't know what this meant, but I knew that God is in control. In the midst of all this and my Facebook fast, on day 3 of the FB fast, I got a text message from a friend of mine from church asking me to talk with her colleague who is facing challenges in her marriage, I got excited and humbled myself before the Lord to use me as he sees fit. Day 4, again after prayer another friend referred her cousin to me who is faced with marital challenges and asked if I can talk with her, praise God. I am ready and willing to walk in my calling! Whatever God wants me to do, I will gladly do it! Praise God for restoring me back to him as my First love by letting go of FB completely. Step by step He will lead us and I choose to follow Him in all of my ways.

Here is another praise report:

The lessons from your ministry made me realize that my life wasn't built on the rock, when my marriage hit a crisis, I crumbled. I looked for help everywhere like pastors, family, friends, etc. Furthermore, I've always been the one who seeks more and more knowledge, and these lessons opened my eyes that I wasn't applying it what I kept learning.

I am now at a point where I'm just seeking God for my life, live His word, to be a living testimony of His goodness. I'm searching the Word to understand what it means to be a Godly woman, a mother, a wife, and a helpmate.

Before coming to RMI I liked to fix or address matters quickly, and this certainly why this led to being contentious. I'm now on a journey to be patient and lean on God fully. I would have divorced my husband the time that he moved out in order to bring an end to this situation, so I thank God for having taught me to be patient and trust Him on this matter. Previously I had put my husband and family first, but right now my Lord is first in my love. I live for Him and He is all I need.

Dear Lord, I want to be the kind of woman you have created me to be, change me and do as you see fit in my life. I've cut off friends as I do not need them to pull me back to my old life. Please and send me new friend to walk this truth within me. Teach me to be polite when I speak, guard my tongue and heart, to always be considerate to the next person.

Ever since I started on the journey to my restoration, I had been looking for something that would help me grow and now I'm at a point in my life where I confidently say nothing is impossible with God.

If I had to say what changed everything, it was that I previously I had put my husband and family first. NOW my Lord is first in my love. As I said, I live for Him, He is all I need.

~ *Busela in South Africa*

*Busela means independent and happy in Zulu

Chapter 29

Catia

"Behold, children are a gift of the Lord;
the fruit of the womb is a reward."
—Psalm 127:3

"Set Off a Forest Fire"

RESTORED Custody

I would like to give praise and thanks to the Lord for how good He has been to me!!! I was asked to share some recent experiences to encourage and motivate those who are seeking the Lord's will through this ministry—especially those of you who have children.

I wanted to tell you that it took me three attempts to get through RYM and it is because I couldn't take my eyes completely off of the circumstances and keep my focus and heart completely on the Lord. The third time around, I finally made up my mind that I was going to finish the third 30 Day attempt successfully and believed that the Lord would bless me with a major breakthrough between my spouse and I. Yes, my eyes were on my restoration and husband too.

I completed the RYM course and the Lord blessed me in many ways. He got rid to the OW, he opened up communication between my spouse and I and he began to ask me what I want and how I want to do things.

He looked forward to when I sent food home to him with the kids. He made sacrifices as to taking the kids to practices and things to make stuff easier on me. We sit next to each other at our kid's sporting events and share laughs and pleasant conversations. In all honesty, I didn't realize just how much the Lord has done for me and my family until I started sharing these things with all of you.

Let me go back to earlier. My marriage is hopeless without God. I am going to paste the email that I sent to your pastors the night I discovered your website by googling a phrase I no longer remember. Forgive the typos.

My husband has left me in a position to fend for myself with no money or support. He has temporary custody of our kids because he made sure that I couldn't make it to court because I was out of state with the kids. I have been staying with a friend, but that is coming to an end. I have been believing God to allow me to go back home. The bible says that "if a wife separates from her husband that she should return home or not remarry...a husband should not divorce his wife." There is no trust left, there is still love from the remnants of 18 years and three children. I am further along in healing than my husband. My love and willingness to trust is returning, while my husband has set his mind on going on with his life without me and has convinced himself that he will not change his mind. Here is the email that I sent you:

hello! my name is catia and i live in new mexico. i just stumbled upon your website and i was impressed. i have asked god to do the impossible in a truly impossible situation. i have been a true believer for the past nine years. my husband of 13 years (18 years of being together) recently filed for divorce.

Ironically, one would think that i should be the one filing. i have been a homemaker for the past 13 years. we have three children and over the past 2-3 years we have gone through a "Job Experience".... my husband used to be a believer, but with all of this, i just don't know anymore.

we were baptized together and my husband was self-employed but has barely made a dime the last five years. we were forced to live off savings and then the inevitable happened. my husband lost all of our money, through investments, and then we lost our home.

well, that was too much for me. I broke after the foreclosure. I would go into hysterics and started calling my husbands names and obscenities and i was angry and downright vicious. i stumbled around like a wounded bear. i stopped believing in God and then my husband. an in-law bought another house for us to live in, but something about the whole thing just didn't feel right to me and i pitched a fit. my husband kept suggesting this neighborhood because there was a family there that he thought we would really get along with and that it was a really cool area, etc. i was lukewarm and too tired to keep fighting.

shortly after moving in we became good friends with that family. hung out almost daily, the wife and i would cook and bake together, well the inevitable with that happened. because our families hung out and our kids were the best of buds, my husband and the neighbor's wife started committing adultery. i knew immediately. i was so sick of my husband and his failures that i turned a blind eye. then i had a change of heart and i exposed him and because of this he overdosed on pills in front of our kids and was taken to the mental hospital.

during the entire time my husband was committing adultery it seemed like some sort of spirit had come over him. our daughter had asked if he was possessed. well as you can imagine, i was heartbroken and my soul was broken because he is my soulmate.

things unraveled quickly. i was so wounded and angry and lashed out in every way that i could, but i still wanted to work on my marriage, but he told me that he couldn't live any of this down and that i would never forgive him. he also said that i was crazy and he didn't want to be married to me anymore. i couldn't believe my ears...

after he was released from the mental hospital my husband and that other woman got back to their adultery again and my husband began to treat me like i was scum on the bottom of his shoe and i would fight back but boy did we both suffer, not to mention the kids. they were even using the kids as pawns to meet up. it was a real mess. he has made it clear that he does not want me. and i have been fighting like a wild cat to hold my family together. please understand that i do love my husband and he loves me, we're just not in love anymore. i hang in there because of our covenant and i want my biological family to stay together and be rebuilt according to God's plan. can you help?

i have been in agony since all of this has happened. I left my husband in july and he sounded so pitiful because he wanted me to bring the kids back home (didn't want me). so I returned with the hopes of reconciliation. but things only got worse. I was convinced he was loosing his mind. he was paranoid and delusional and completely irrational in his thinking and behavior. he was hiding keys and medicine bottles in a safe he had hidden in the house. we were living in a house of horrors. i was so worried abut my husband because he kept threatening me with divorce and kicking me out of his relative's house. I finally had him recommitted to the mental hospital. he had blocked my communication with his relatives so i was left on my own. the next day, his father, who is an attorney, got my husband released on an outpatient basis and they went to and filed divorce papers. my husband stayed away form the house for a couple of days and showed up with his father and a witness from the courts to watch him pack his stuff while my husband and his father announced in front our children that he was divorcing me for committing "perjury." i had never heard such a farce in my life. and the damage done to our kids... so the next day, i packed up my truck with as much as i could and took my kids and went back to my home state. we were settling in and thriving. then i was served with divorce papers with a demand for me to show up to court 17 days later. it was impossible for me to make it. i had sick kids, etc. because I didn't go, my husband won temporary orders by default. i filed for a motion of rehearing because i was blocked from our finances and it took me a little longer to get an attorney. that's when my husband came to where we were and snatched to kids out of school with the sheriff and it caused them so much trauma, our daughter has been having stomach problems and was being treted for depression. she sneeked an email to tell me about it. her dad told the kids they cannot talk or interact with me without his permission. this is an impossible mess. you know, i was really believing for this marriage until i started to fathom the things that i am writing right now. i have suffered extreme mental and emotional abuse from that man and he accuses me of being the same way.

i have been asking god to just stop the divorce and deal with us while his covenant is upheld. we have no history of any of this stuff. i believe the financial pressures did us in. in the mean time i realized my husband was seeking legal counsel behind my back. he would tell me that he didn't know what he was going to do and start blaming me for everything. i also discovered that he had gone to our children's school and had started to build his case against me to convince them that i was unstable.

so I'm writing to ask, do you really think i should keep believing for this? maybe my husband is right. maybe we should do our own thing. i am appalled by all of this. an hour ago i was praising god for our recovery, renewal and restoration.

my husband insisted that i didn't work and that he had everything under control, every other week he was going to have a $15 million IPO. my downfall is that i was seriously in love with my husband and believed everything and anything that he told me.

this same relative who bought the house has been taking care of us for the past 3 years, and his family, has taken all accountability and responsibility from him and had justified his behavior. they have only listened to his side of things (lots of lies) and have blamed me for everything. we are a mixed couple and i know that even though they expressed love and kindness to a degree i was always tolerated for the sake of my husband. they got him a nanny for the kids. yes, that relative is wealthy.

i just wanted my husband to be the man and me take care our kids and our home. i wrote a letter recently to that relative asking her to pray about her involvement in our marital affairs. i assured her that i was not what i was being made out to be and that the family really needed to look at the fact that my husband isn't well. i asked her to pray about things and to keep her house and her money and for his family to back off and to let us figure things out on their own. i told her if they really wanted to help him then suggest marriage counseling or going back to put his family together.

sincerely,
videogirl

Many of you are probably thinking that no one's situation is like yours...you haven't read anything that compares. Here is some food for thought...allow me to share with you a big part of why it took me three tries to get through and why I am grateful for how much He has already restored. I have to admit that things between my spouse and me are good. Communication is so much better. Negative emotions have pretty much evaporated on my part and he is doing so much better. He is pleasant to me and answers questions instead of grunting at me. I even get smiles sometimes. We have increased phone conversations and when occasionally have long ones, we end up having some good laughs together. My husband has been opening up to some things going on in his personal life and he has gotten so much better about making me feel welcome when I am at the house.

A couple of times I even caught him peeking around the corner at me. I pretended I didn't see him. We were at one of our kids sporting events and I was talking to an old friend. My husband was standing on the other side of that friend, but didn't see me yet. When he realized it was me, he looked at me as if I were beautiful. Please forgive me for not sending in any praise reports that I have had over the past few months. I do believe when the Lord is ready for me to submit them, people will be wowed and inspired.

For the past week, the Lord has been giving me scripture telling me that I am married. However, he blew m socks off yesterday. I was SG in terms of employment and I cried out to the Lord to send me a solid Word that would help me. He showed me Psalms 107:20 NASB. I prayed that scripture back to Him and about 40 minutes later, I had the urge to pick up my bible to meditate on a promise. I never made it to that scripture. Instead my bible opened to Isaiah 62. The word "married" jumped out at me. (To speed things up), the Lord said that He has changed my name and delights in me and that "my land" is "married". I was blown away!!! I just switched from NLT to NASB in March 2014. this is what the NASB bible says:

It will no longer be said to you, "Forsaken,"

Nor to your land will it any longer be said, "Desolate";

But you will be called, "My delight is in her,"

And your land, "Married";

For the Lord delights in you, And to Him your land will be married.

Why this scripture is so special is that I had read some marriage testimony a couple of years ago and the Lord had given the woman this scripture and soon after, her marriage was fully restored. I had never seen that translation before—so I said to myself, "If the Lord sees fit to give me that same scripture then I KNOW that my marriage is fully restored." The other thing is that the biggest promise that I have been truly meditating on are twin scriptures Jeremiah 30:10-11 (NLT), 17-18. Verse 17 states that I was an outcast, whom no one cared about; the Lord has turned things around in the spiritual and natural. I am expecting that suddenly any moment.

Things are not perfect, but my thinking and demeanor has changed so much. It is funny—I am right back in the same crisis as a year ago with no job! Now, I don't care. I have faith in God to guide and provide. I do love to minister to women with marriage difficulties, but in all honesty, I haven't had many opportunities lately.

All I can say is God bless, Erin— I am finally got it! I simply seek the Lord and trust Him with everything. I have learned to cease from striving. I wait on the Lord!!!! I have no interest in discussing things with anyone. I don't want others opinions. When I first applied for an ePartner—I was like, great!!!! It didn't take long to figure out that I didn't need one. I have no interest to pick up the phone. I quit a minimum wage job last year, which I loved and thrived in, to take this last position because I was listening to "other people" telling me I had to take care of myself. I felt pressure because I have been staying with a friend and I naturally wanted my own place. The Lord had me where He wanted me and I blew it because I was trying to figure things out. I got the new job and none of its promises manifested, I ended up making far less money because I got out of God's will. God's plans are bigger and better. I learned my lesson and now, I wait on the Lord.

Erin is so anointed and she is so correct in her teachings and I truly love you guys. I noticed a few weeks ago that I hadn't me the conditions of God's promise to me until recently. "Do not be afraid or discouraged..." I have learned that while I wait, He works. This time last year, I had taken my attention off of everything and the Lord was moving the OW clear across the country. My guess is that the Lord is using this crisis to send me home. Praise God! He has been so faithful. The other thing is that He would tell me each place that I would land before I got there and that is exactly where I would go. I do believe that I have taken possession. I'm going home. No more wilderness wanderings (yes, I have a filled out my journal about all of this). These past few months, the Lord has given me and my mother dreams about reconciliation and they have all been prophetic. We both have similar spiritual gifts. I cannot wait to submit my restored marriage testimony.

The other thing is that the marriage stuff really isn't my focus. I find myself shrugging my shoulders on stuff, where in the past I would've been upset. I am so excited about the love I know have! I hear the Lord and He sees and hears me. Ladies, this goes for All of us!!!! That thrills me—my relationship with the Lord. I must have finally gotten with His program because He delights in me. I am thrilled and so in love with the Lord. God is working and He won't waste my prayers. I do believe that I will be your next restoration testimony. Whew!!!! So sorry. Excited to have contact with the ministry.

Something else I need to confess. I did something "out of love" (I believed my husband's behavior really did warrant what I did) and I put my spouse back in the mental hospital. Sadly (because I didn't let God do it) it was twisted around and set off a forest fire, and to retaliate, my EH and his entire family, including the OW, did their best to take my kids from me.

They were able to get a phony arrest warrant issued from another state to have me expedited out of my current state and it included about 15 trumped up charges on me stating that I was a drug dealer, I was armed and dangerous and a whole bunch of other things that I didn't even know existed.

They thought that no one would ever help me or believe me and that I would lose everything and everyone that was dear to me. From the world's perspective that looked like a real possibility. I was in jail for 10 days and the first three days I didn't even know why.

Without knowing or asking, my employer and his wife immediately hired an attorney and the Lord used them to clear me from everything. It turns out that I was arrested over a $3.98 prescription, for a "controlled substance." The day I got out of jail I went home and that same bottle of pills was in my bathroom drawer over 1/2 filled of the same pills in its original container, which was prescribed to me by my husband's first cousin (an ER doctor) who had written an RX for me 2 years prior on a family trip. He told me to fill out the RX pad and he would sign it.

Well, I did and attempted to fill it when the pharmacist noticed it wasn't signed. So, we tried to reach the "Dr." by phone and he didn't answer- it was no big deal to me. He simply called it in that evening to another pharmacy. I thought that was the end of the story. That small thing was what the enemy used as a trump card to destroy me. My father in law is an attorney and I am positive that he was used by the enemy too.

Soon after the Lord released me, as I sought Him, things began to go not so well for any of those who so diligently worked against. As it is written one reaps what they sow. Believe me when I tell you that the Reapers have caught up with the Sowers.

[Keep in mind, anyone who knows me knows that I have never participated in drugs, smoking or heavy drinking. Praise the Lord- I have never had the appetite for those things.]

And as He says, all things work together for good. Remember how I said there was no one for me to minister to? Well, that's why He put me there. While in jail, I ministered to the women there and 98.9% of the women were in jail due to a man they wanted back—me included. The Lord used me mightily as I soon recognized He sent me there on assignment, to share the truth I had learned from this ministry and how I ended up in jail. The confirmation was these women told me later that they thought I was an angel and that what I said to them was answers to their prayers.

While in jail, I was torn. I felt a deep sadness over how much hatred my EH must have had in his heart towards me. I found myself asking the Lord, "Do you still want me to believe You for this marriage?"

So now let me tell you the details and how God brought me through this. It was clear even to the arresting officers that something was amiss. I was held in some observation room all by myself for about 4 hrs. I knew I hadn't done anything and I knew the Lord was with me, so I just fell asleep.

Finally, around 3 AM I was led to my cell and something in my spirit said whatever cell that you get that's how long I would be in jail. I was told I would be on the second floor so the first cell I saw was 3. I smiled to myself and said " I can handle 3 days- Jesus did!" The guard then told me that I would be going to cell 10. Gulp!!!

On day 10 we were put back in our cells to prepare for dinner. I thought to myself, "Lord, I know that I heard You correctly. The courts closed 30 min ago and now we are on lock down for dinner. How am I going to get out of here now? You said, 10 days!"

Lo and behold, about 30 minutes later my name was called to go home! No one knows how or why this was done!!! The next day I left town to start my new job, while my attorney showed up to court not knowing where his client was or how I got released.

While in jail, I read this little book called, "Those who trust in the Lord will not be disappointed." To this day I lean heavily on that biblical promise. It works!! I also give testimony to this.

It was on my third day in jail that I cried out to the Lord to tell me *why* I was in jail. I knew I hadn't done anything. About 15 min into prayer, I heard this small voice STATE THE LEGAL NAME of my RX. Then it all came to me what had been conspired! I knew the Lord had His plan for me being there, so I submitted to Him and He has consistently blessed me and helped along the way.

I need to tell you that when I was released from jail, it was as if everyone in the cell block knew before me that I was leaving. When my name was called and I stood in front of the cell window so that the guard could see me.

I saw all of the women on both floors standing looking out their windows waving and crying. There wasn't a dry eye in the place. They were applauding me and wishing me well.

I could hear them through those thick, concrete walls. This is when I knew that I had to trust the Lord no matter what things looked like. I'd gone where He wanted me to take the Good News, to free all of those women who were obsessed with a man, so they could hear about a Man who would love them.

After I left, just last week I had only little money in the bank and I had to choose to get my car payment to prevent repossession or pay my rent. I made the decision to pay the car and trust God for the rent. I kid you not-Jesus walked on water that day. I paid my car and 15 min after I got home the leasing office called to tell me that my rent check came back as a closed account. I just told them that I would take care of it and we figured out that I had given them the wrong checking account—an honest mistake. I got on my knees to pray.

Thirty minutes later I remembered that I had promised the Lord that I would begin checking my bank account daily. Lo and behold the $500 that I had taken out was in my account!! There was no record of the car payment. The car transaction had cleared my account the day before. It was not a pending transaction-the balances reflected as much.

So I got up, went to the bank and got a money order for my rent. I wasn't about to trust a debit card or another check transaction. Praise God! He got my rent paid in full and my car payment made. My little mind was swimming for days.

I know this is long, but what I want everyone to take away from my testimony is that it is crucial to share your faith with your kids. My kids cherish and honor me, especially now because of all that has happened and in their eyes I have not wavered in my faith.

Also to focus on Him and move through the courses so you are ready for what may be up ahead. And that no matter what, God will use whatever trial for GOOD if you trust Him to see you through. If you don't share your testimony with everyone around you, helping other women, He will be sure to put you where women need to hear it the most, like He did with me.

No matter what, the most important thing to know is that God is faithful and pours out His unfailing love on all of us though His son our Heavenly Husband.

TRUST HIM. BELIEVE HIM AND KNOW THAT HE IS THE GOD OF THE IMPOSSIBLE.

~ *Catia in New Mexico*

Cheryl

"He makes the barren woman
Abide in the house
As a joyful mother of children.
Praise the LORD!"
—Psalm 113:9

"There is No Secret Formula"

To all you women without children - God wants to restore your marriage. And to all you women in the UK - God lives here too...!

I was only married for 6 months when it just turned even more sour and nasty by the day and I kept telling myself "This is not my happy Christian marriage I signed up for."

There were constant battles about money, housework, differences in opinions and crockery flying. We never went to church because we were falling away. I found out things about my husband that made me tell him I was ashamed I married him and I would scoff that I'd never be able to bring children into our marriage, how much I hated him and that everyone told me never to marry him.

Then I eventually was so exhausted and had enough of fights that I told him I was leaving, I'd had enough of this marriage, and he also would have to find somewhere else to live. This in turn led to a fight that turned nasty and the police had to intervene.

Well, I was all for filing for divorce and starting again, maybe even being single the rest of my life. A life of quiet sounded like bliss. But one day I am sure I felt God tell me He wanted to restore my marriage and I was to pursue this. O.K.?! I searched for all the scriptures on marriage I knew and had to have it confirmed - God's will for my marriage. I must say that God gave me a good telling off for my contentious behaviour and taught me many lessons. However, He is a gentle forgiving Father.

Nobody was with me. Not my Christian parents, who gave me "what for?" and said "best of luck with that!", when I told them God was going to restore my marriage. My Christian friends tried their best but after a few glasses of wine, gave me the sympathetic head tilt...apparently God doesn't do that!

So I learned I just had to shut up. This was my journey to go alone...me and My God. And eventually I came across your ministry. Which confirmed everything and which I must admit, I devoured in a whole 7 days - then had to let my brain cool down.

Up to this point I had zero contact with my husband or his family, didn't even know where he was. I felt in my heart I had to write to him and apologise for my part in events. This didn't sit well in my mind as the material says NEVER to contact them. But it kept stirring in me and I prayed for favour and after a few days, I just had to do it. This letter opened up the doors of communication and we have spoken via SMS every day and met up for a couple weekends away.

In our time apart, God has been talking to my husband too and he has returned to church and has been listening to Christian radio and praying and declaring. WOW...talk about "exceedingly and abundantly beyond all I can ever imagine..."

Husband is due to come home to live tomorrow...Praise GOD! We have a court case to go through first which is not nice but unavoidable and the enemy is trying his best to intimidate...he knows his time is up! But I know who goes before me and has prepared the way. A new journey starts from here.

My advice is that there is no secret formula when it comes to the things of God. You only have to remember who's your Daddy?! The King of Kings. What does that make you? A PRINCESS. An heiress with all authority in your hands and the enemy under your feet. God knows you. He made you. He loves you and wants to heal your life. Take all the RMI has to offer, and then make sure His truth doesn't stay a secret and share the Good News with everyone!!

~ *Cheryl in Scotland*

Ministry Note: We were thrilled that Cheryl listened to the Lord who led her to contact her husband. The truth is, in the RYM book it says that if YOU are the one who left or kicked your husband out, then you ARE to be the one to contact your husband not wait for him. The "no contact" is for the majority of women whose husbands have left on their own accord.

Chapter 31

Phyllis

"Behold, children are a gift of the Lord;
the fruit of the womb is a reward."
—Psalm 127:3

"RESTORED in Vermont"

Looking at us on the surface, people thought my husband and I were the "perfect" couple. However, those who looked deep into our souls knew there was something wrong. I never really seemed or felt happy. My EARTHLY HUSBAND showered me with so much love and affection, yet it wasn't enough. I rarely reciprocated it, and at times I felt smothered. Because I never knew how to be in an intimate relationship with my Heavenly Husband, I wasn't able to be in one with my earthly husband. Even my relationship with my heavenly Husband seemed "perfect" to those on the outside looking in, but I and my heavenly Husband knew better.

I always received so much from both my heavenly Husband and my EH, yet I only gave part of me. I had a void inside of me dating back to my teen and college years that I tried to fill with my marriage, job titles, volunteering, owning a business, just to name a few. After the long journey to motherhood and the birth of our son, I became detached, aloof, and fell into a depression. While on maternity leave, I fell victim to a ravenous wolf - false teaching of well-publicized pastor. I acted as if I didn't want to be bothered with my husband. Eventually, we became roommates sleeping in separate rooms and living separate lives.

The Lord warned me so many times that I needed to change; to grow up and be the woman, wife and mother Christ needed me to be for Him and my husband. My earthly husband told me on many occasions that one day he was going to wake up and not feel the same anymore. My mother would often tell me that I needed to close my business and focus on my marriage. However, I wanted my ears tickled and knew that I could have it all. I ignored all the warning signs. The Lord continued to warn me 2 to 3 months prior to the fall of my marriage. Three months prior to my journey, my Love warned me through a dream where I lied on the ground motionless and covered with grey snakes.

I was disturbed from this dream, but not enough to seek wisdom in its meaning (until after the fact). In God's agape love for me, He gave me a final warning when my earthly husband called me crying out to me. He said he was willing to give up all of his projects and business pursuits, renew our vows, and try for another child for us to be close again. I consoled him and said ok, but the next day I did not change. A month later, the Lord sent a big fish to swallow me up and 'removed my lover and friend far from me.' I was truly in darkness, alone. Now my Savior finally had my attention.

The next few days, I searched for advice online. Nothing really talked to my soul. I went to my Christian mother's online support board for advice. Everyone on the board had plenty of answers and opinions, but none of them seemed like THE answer. One of the mothers sent me a private message with a link to the first chapter of How God Can and Will Restore Your Marriage. I read the first chapter, and I began to cry. I purchased the e-version of the book, and immediately began to read it within 2 to 3 days.

The scales were removed from my eyes. I finally saw myself how God saw me and it wasn't pretty. I was spoiled, self-centered, and immature who thought I had it all together. After finishing the book and sending in my marriage evaluation to take the courses, a weight was immediately lifted off of my shoulders.

I realized that my heavenly Husband had something better planned for my life than my plan. For the first time in my life, I was not only full of hope, but also my void was being filled with the love of Christ.

I learned that I needed an intimate relationship with my heavenly Husband— it is how He designed us and what both He and I want and needed. I truly learned what a Christian marriage looks like, which should mimic our relationship with Christ. I understood what it meant to be a quiet and gentle spirit. I recognized and deeply understood my role as a Bride to my heavenly Husband, a wife to my EH, and a mother to my son. As outlined so beautifully in the RMI courses and books, I let go of those things that were holding me back - Facebook, emails, my marriage, certain friendships, my business, the house, my church. The more I let go and let God, the more my tears began to dry up. My life was being destroyed right in front of my eyes for a new one.

It wasn't easy to let go of all the things that I was familiar with. But I knew I had to, for my heavenly Husband, myself and my marriage. The most difficult times that God helped me through was seeing my husband's affections towards someone else. My earthly husband became emotionally attached to someone else. The more I clung to my First Love, it seemed like the more my husband clung to the OW.

They were times when I was shown signs that my earthly husband was spending time with the OW for hours, but as Erin tells us, I kept it to myself and continued to look into the face of my heavenly Husband. There were times when my earthly husband would send me nasty texts telling me that he wanted to leave and make a new life with the OW or tell me to leave him alone. It was those times I cried unto the Lord asking Him to "take this cup from me if Thy will", but I knew the answer. The worse was when my earthly husband called me in hysteria, sounding suicidal. I was frozen with fear, but I knew the Lord was calling me to Be Still.

I remained still and continued to read my 3x5 cards over and over again. I received three more calls from my earthly husband in succession, each time with him sounding worse than before. I was tempted to call my EH's mother and siblings, but I knew the Lord wanted me to Be Still, which I did. Eventually, it passed and the Lord showed me that my earthly husband was just fine. I walked through this fiery furnace with the Father, Son and Holy Spirit right next to me, PTL.

The turning point of my restoration was several months after I walked through the fiery furnace. My earthly husband never moved out, as he wanted to do, the OW became bitter as wormwood before my eyes, and the walls were completely down. My heavenly Husband began allowing my earthly husband and I to date again, with date nights to the movies, lunch or dinner, fitness club, and even a weekend away without our son.

Prior to Lent, the Lord placed upon my heart that He wanted me to go on a 40-Day Daniel Fast. During this time, I got deeper into His Word. I took my 3x5 cards and did an in depth Bible study on them - one per night. He directed me to reread certain chapters of the Wise Woman Book - Gentle and Quiet Spirit, Winning Without a Word and Created Female. Yes, I did read these chapter before, but I didn't go deeper - I didn't truly act upon these chapters. The Lord also directed me to read other books and devotionals that were in line with Wise Woman and Workers at Home Books that emphasized how to be the kind of wife the Lord needed me to be for my EH. I found that I was enjoying this intimate time with my heavenly Husband and looked forward to it.

The Lord gave me many dreams and the power to interpret these dreams. I would have the same dream involving trying to cross murky waters for a few months. During my fast, the Lord gave me this dream again, but only this time, the water was calm and clear and I wasn't afraid to cross the bridge.

After seeking wisdom, I realized the Lord wanted me to step out on faith and take the next step in my journey in truly becoming the wife He needed for me to be.

I was fearful at first, but realized I couldn't go wrong with God on my side. Plus, I had already buried my dear sister Fear and eulogized her in October through a praise report. The more intimate and obedient I became with my heavenly Husband, the closer my earthly husband and I became. We began sharing our most intimate thoughts which each other. Because I was able to share these things with my heavenly Husband first, it became easy for me to share them with my EH.

Just a couple of weeks ago, my spouse and I were with our son at the store. He mentioned our 15th wedding anniversary in August. I said yes I know, not thinking anything of it.

My earthly husband continued and said that we had been through a lot and we needed to celebrate it by going away. I don't think I realized what he said because my focus was now on the Lord. It took a while for my EH's statement to process. Unlike our wedding 15 years ago, this time, we will be renewing our vows on a Caribbean beach with Christ at the center, me, my EH, the preacher with NEW rings symbolizing the new life in Christ for our marriage.

I cannot even begin to express how wonderful RMI's resources are to ALL women, no matter what their marital status is. No ministry that I came across when I was in darkness provided the type of spiritual guidance, truth and support I needed for this journey. The RYM book gave me the foundation for my new life with all Biblical principles. By Word of Their Testimony, the Daily Encourager, and my e-Partner/friend (thank God for her) provided me with the support and encouragement I needed to go on. The Wise Woman and Workers at Home Book allowed me to go deeper into His Word. Every day I thank God for Erin's blind obedience to God to carry out His Master Plan of this ministry. I hope that I can be just as encouraging to others, as others have been to me.

Ladies, please remember that God hand picked each one of us. It is no accident that we have all found ourselves on this road, entering through this narrow gate.

"Enter through the narrow gate; for the gate is wide and the way is broad that leads to destruction, and there are many who enter through it. For the gate is small and the way is narrow that leads to life, and there are few who find it." (Matthew 7:13-14). Don't just stay outside of the gate peeking in. Enter in to see what's behind it. Yes, it's painful at times, and lonely and dark, but well worth it. Use this time to get closer to our heavenly Husband. The only way to find true happiness, contentment and to live life abundantly is through our heavenly Husband. C.S. Lewis, a Christian author once wrote "Don't shine so others can see you. Shine so that through you, others can see Him."

Allow God to be your all and everything so that your light can shine and others can see us through Him.

"Vows Renewed with Christ at the Center"

"For I know the plans I have for you,' declares the Lord, 'plans to prosper you and not to harm you, plans to give you hope and a future.'" Jeremiah 29:11 (NIV)

Well I had no idea what plans my heavenly Husband had for my vow renewal/anniversary celebration to my EH. I was so nervous the week prior to our departure and the minutes leading up to my vow renewal to my EH; even more nervous than the first time we got married. But I knew that my Beloved could not fail! This anniversary was truly about love. "Whoever does not love does not know God, because God is love: 1 John 4:8 (NIV). Unlike before, this time I truly knew God and thus I knew about love for both my heavenly Husband and EH.

My heavenly Husband planned the PERFECT destination second honeymoon for us. Perfect in every way. Even the best wedding planner money could buy would never be able to top what my First Love planned.

I want to take you back into time with me 15 years ago so you will understand the magnitude of my Love's perfect plan for this celebration.

Fifteen years ago, my wedding was not about my heavenly Husband 's love for me or my love for my EH. It was a production. Twenty-five people in the bridal party with over 110 guests, many of whom neither I nor my earthly husband speak to anymore. I never considered what my Beloved wanted for me. I couldn't even enjoy the day; everything felt rushed. The honeymoon was more like a vacation between two best friends rather than a time to become closer to my heavenly Husband and my EH. This set the tone for my marriage for years to come. A life full of selfishness and no sacrifice.

Fast forward to today, my Love left no detail unnoticed and gave us the most beautiful and intimate ceremony and second honeymoon - a Caribbean destination. When my earthly husband and I initially contacted the resort about conducting our vow renewal, they gave a brochure with packages that were way more than we knew we needed to spend and with things that we didn't need.

We asked the resort three separate times about the fee, in hopes that since we didn't want anything elaborate, we wouldn't be charged so much. The answer was always the same. Even the photographer we contacted wanted a fee that was just as much as the resort's anniversary package. Then my Beloved whispered, "Don't worry. I have everything all taken care of. "So my earthly husband and I left without knowing the details for anything - not even the exact day, time or location.

But oh, my Beloved knew and had everything under control! Prior to our departure, I received wedding gifts that I did not even expect. He arranged for us to have private transportation to the resort at no additional cost with early check-in, though we were initially told that our room wouldn't be ready when we arrived.

The weather was picture perfect. Our room directly overlooked the wedding gazebo leading to the beach, and I knew at that moment that my heavenly Husband wanted us to renew our vows right at that gazebo. (Every day, I sat on the balcony and became even closer to my heavenly Husband through reading His word and writing).

We were even able to book a photo session with the resort's photographer at 85% less than if we'd booked with the other photographer! There were so many details that my heavenly Husband provided for us that every time I or my earthly husband noticed it, we both were praising Him!

When my heavenly Husband revealed the time, day and location that our vow renewal was to take place, there was not a single soul around. Normally, the wedding gazebo is used by the resort for wedding ceremonies (bride's walk to the beach for the ceremony). When we arrived, there were a few ceremonies going on, but on our special day ordained by my Beloved, the wedding gazebo remained unused!!

My earthly husband and I sat underneath that gazebo overlooking the ocean and exchanged our written vows to each other with God as the preacher. He even provided us with witnesses as a few of the guests viewed us exchanging vows from their rooms. It was the most beautiful and intimate ceremony, which was focused on spiritual and not earthly things. My Love even provided us with a small cake in our room afterwards, and an intimate wedding reception!

The best part of this whole destination second honeymoon is not the location or the wedding gifts. It's not even the vows that my earthly husband and I exchanged, though that was wonderful. The day before our departure and official anniversary, my earthly husband gave his testimony to family and friends of his restoration journey and how God has been moving in his life. He testified that because I showed him unconditional love, it helped him to look at himself and change.

So many couples reached out to both of us sharing their own journeys, and letting us know how our testimonies inspired them! Ladies, I say this not to boast because none of this was done by us. I say this to state that my Beloved chose me to be the sacrificial lamb; to go ahead of family and friends and pave the way for them to experience His intimacy, mercy, grace and plans; in other words, His best for them.

When I was at my worst point last year, my Beloved was at His best not only working in me, but working in my earthly husband and others that I love. My journey, and yours, is a part of our heavenly Husband 's master plan to bring Him all the glory and honor, and to bring others closer to Him. "Not only so, but we also rejoice in our sufferings, because we know that suffering produces perseverance; perseverance, character; and character, hope. And hope does not disappoint us, because God has poured out His love into our hearts by the Holy Spirit, whom He has given us." Romans 5:3-5 (NIV)

~ Phyllis in Vermont is a new Minister in Training who has encouraged all of us through her enthusiasm and AMAZING praise reports. Like almost all of us, she believed the world's lies about marriage until her husband had had enough. Then began this great journey with the Lord where she changed into who you will get to know and love as we all have. Most recently Phyllis has been on ministry sabbatical after writing children's book.

———————Chapter 32———————

Hanna

"Behold, children are a gift of the Lord;
the fruit of the womb is a reward."
—Psalm 127:3

"If You Will Wait!"

My husband left me a year ago in June. He left very suddenly and didn't want much to do with me. I was extremely hurt and immediately sought after God.

After about a month God told me to love my husband unconditionally. I tried (in my own strength) to do that and we kind of got back together for about a month. But I was still the same contentious woman wanting everything my own way. My husband started pulling away again.

I love and respect my Pastor and his wife, they are godly people but they advised me to cut off intimacy with him (at this time there was no OW). I did and then my EH really pulled away from me. They also said to confront him and push him into reconciling or divorce. I did, and he said that he did want a divorce but he didn't want to hurt me. He wanted to divorce with no attorney, I said that I would think about it but I didn't think I trusted him enough to do that. Then a woman called my work (I had never spoken to her before), and somehow she told me about RMI. She invited me over to her house to borrow her materials that night. God bless you Debbie, you were used of God. Don't forget that!!!!

As I read How God can and will Restore your Marriage, God began convicting me about my own pride, unrealistic expectations, and judgment that I had heaped upon my husband for 11 years! I was broken. God showed me how to seek Him and His word through that book. The Encouragement tapes and the testimony book enabled me to hope for what I thought was hopeless. God taught me about hope and faith and unconditional love. I realize now that He had been trying to teach me for years but I couldn't understand or imagine the depth of any of those things, although I sought Him. I started loving my husband no matter what he did or didn't do. I started putting all my expectations and hope in the Lord only.

As I sought God, however, things got worse. The RYM warns us this will happen and not to be shaken. My world shook as I discovered there was another woman. Day by day went by with no hope, no affection from my EH. Nevertheless, day-by-day, God filled me with hope in Him and with HIS affection and HIS love showered on me as He became my everything. I'm thankful for this time because I learned to lean on Him only. What a miracle. I cannot even begin to tell you all the prayers that He answered even though I stopped praying for things. Little ones like having my husband offer to set up my computer (when others had offered--I waited!). Big ones like knowing how to handle talking to my kids about the OW. Just resting in my HH changed everything in my life.

God taught me that the key to seeking Him is to love and meditate on His word, to breathe it in day and night and sense Him next to me. Let the songs you listen to be songs that speak of His love, regular love songs not religious ones, also, asking Him to remove the desire to watch or read love stories that would tempt me to take my mind off of HIM and back on my EH. Only watch what He leads me to, watching things as a couple, just me and Him! It's not impossible ladies! And this is what taught me to wait for His answers!! As we discussed everything, He told me this over and over throughout the Bible, through songs, through the RMI materials and website, and through Streams in the Desert, which I read daily.

If you put Him first, make Him your First Love and speak to Him as if He is right next to you—He will answer if you will wait. He promises us that as His bride!!!

He taught me that it is O.K. to hope in Him. It is safe. It is assured. It is wonderful to speak in faith. It blesses Him. He will show you great and mighty things that you do not know just as Erin says. God assured me that He knows what is best for me. He wants my future to be filled with love for Him.

When I found out about the OW, which was confirmed, by a comment made by my 8 year old, immediately the darkness began to engulf me. I wanted to give up, and sadly I even spoke it out loud. But then, He would not allow me to continue to feel this way. That is the weekend that I experienced the peace that passes all understanding in a depth that was new to me!! After that peace came, one week later my husband told me that he loved me and he missed our kids and he wanted to come home. Isn't that amazing? Once He knew I was His, and that I would come to Him for everything, He turned my husband's heart back, just as Erin and all the lessons say will happen.

When my EH came over, he admitted to me there was an OW and that he wanted out, but he was trapped. It was sudden. Again everything RMI says will happen and what's happening that we know nothing about. Even though I thought it was over and was fine with just me and my HH, He had it all planned. Two weeks went by and I heard nothing personally from my EH, but I was fine with just my HH. Then I found out he had moved in with the OW, next he started introducing her to his family, yet my HH held me up and more than ever I felt His love. And what's amazing is that by the grace of my Lord, I continued to love my husband unconditionally channeling the Love I got from my HH.

Shortly after he moved in with the other woman, he then gave me the divorce papers. At this point most women would abandon restoration, but that's not how He works. He leads us though the valley, wanting to be right by our side. And this is when He covered me with more grace and mercy and love for my husband and the OW. Isn't that remarkable? Remember this is a process of cleansing us, removing every trace of our EH being first in our lives, where HE is the center of our everything. I won't lie and say there weren't gut-wrenching tears and failures and prayers that seemed unanswered in between all these highs, but each time I found myself closer and closer to Him.

There were sweet things my HH did for me too, like when my husband cried when he handed me the papers. And how I was able to shower him with reassurance of my love that I knew he needed. I hugged him. I told him that he was an awesome dad and had been a much better husband than I was a wife to him! Trust me, that was not me. That was Jesus using a broken vessel to pour out His love on a lost sheep! Every time a new paper would have to be signed (custody, court release) I smiled and didn't question. I didn't fight anything he wanted. Then a few months later he gave me the final paper. It was over. I was sad. I wept. But my HH gave me hope and more hope and I again remembered He was all I wanted anyway.

It was about a week after the divorce was final when my husband unexpectedly came by to put the kids to bed (he had never done that during the year he was gone). He started weeping and I walked him outside and talked to him to comfort him, saying everything would be alright. He started talking about me and how much he loved me and how he missed his kids so much. He said his life was ruined, he was in major debt and there was no hope for him. He said that there was no way he could leave this woman although he wanted me more than anything! And as prompted, I spoke about God's hope (very gently) to soothe him

I told him he was welcome home any time (which I had told him many times before when he would ask). I reassured him of my love. I was amazed at this personal conversation and at the amazing amount of affection from my EH. Does God answer exceedingly, abundantly beyond all that you can think or imagine? Yes! Yes! Yes! My husband left suddenly that night, without a word, but I praised the Lord for hours after he left. Later that night, the phone rang. It was my husband asking if he could spend the night on my couch. I said, "Of course." We talked all that night!!! And he stayed a full month before we found out there was still one divorce paper that was never filed correctly!! Praise God, the divorce didn't go through as either of us thought, and all I can say is ONLY GOD could do that!!!!

My situation was hopeless; it looked like my husband was happy. It looked like he was set to his course no matter his distress at hurting me and leaving our children. But God tells us not to believe what we see. So ladies, do as RMI says, let go of your husband, put the Lord, your HH first, and when things then begin to get worse, get closer to Him, don't turn back to being unfaithful with your EH first. Your EH will need HIS love that can come through you.

God says that He fights this battle for us whether we see the battle or not! God says to believe His promises and receive His blessings. God says to wait on Him only!

~ *Hanna in Oklahoma*

Chapter 33

Jean Luc

"Behold, children are a gift of the Lord;
the fruit of the womb is a reward."
—Psalm 127:3

"Restored in Mauritius""

Jean Luc please tell our readers, how your marriage crisis began:

My wife was very distant with me for about 10 month. We were like two strangers in our house. She didn't talk to me. She pass all her time at her mother's house. We were not intimate. And I was drunk a lot because of this situation.

Next, Jean Luc, please tell our readers, how did God change you & your situation as you sought Him wholeheartedly?

After coming here I began to pray and fast twice in a week, I began to read the Holy Bible, and I stopped drinking. That's when I began to have faith in my difficult situation knowing He could restore us.

Jean Luc can you please tell our readers, what principles, from God's Word (or through our resources), that the Lord taught you during this trial?

Most important that I learned right away is that Nothing is impossible for God. Also, that we walk by faith not by sight because we all expect to see some change when He says we won't because that's not faith. Very important to repent of your sins. Not until I repented of all my sins and turned away from them did I find faith. And that the reason He asks us to go through this trial is that God wanted to teach me humility.

Please tell our readers, Jean Luc, what your most difficult times were that God helped you through.

When I knew that my wife was in adultery. Then soon after, the other man came to talk to me and did so violently. The worse was because my son witness all these scenes each time it happened.

Jean Luc, please help our readers know if you suspected you were close to restoration? Were there any signs?

No i suspected nothing. Again we need to live by faith when we see no change.

Now Jean Luc please tell our readers what was the "turning point" of your restoration?

The turning point for me is when I felt like a great peace came over me in this hopeless situation. Soon after my wife began to be sick, and then one day she sent me an email. In it, she said she didn't know what to do, she felt like a great guilt had overtaken her soul and she couldn't pray anymore. Just like it says in RMI's materials for men, that if we do what He asks and we make Him first, following all the principles that are designed to change us into the husband we need to be for our wives, then God will create a crisis in our wife's life in order for her to come to us.

Jean Luc if you would, carefully explain just HOW it happened: Did your wife contact you by phone or just show up at your home?

One early morning my wife showed up at my home, soon after she emailed. We talked a lot and then I felt I needed to tell her to come back home. She quickly said yes, but she also said she was very afraid. So a few more days passed, I was simply patient knowing God had to finish it. Even though she didn't come home then, we continued emailing each other, then even to laugh together, then one Saturday I asked her to stay. That day she accepted and since then, she has been safely in our home and I am able to be the husband she always needed me to be.

Lastly, Jean Luc, based on your own restoration, would you recommend any of our resource in particular that helped you?

By the Word of Their Testimony and the *Be Encouraged eVideos* were very helpful in my restoration. I also recommend these below because all these resources for men will help anyone who is in a very hopeless marriage. I know they work to change men and restored their marriages.

How God Will Restore your Marriage
A Wise Man
By the Word of Their Testimony
Facing Divorce
Daily Devotionals
Encourager
Be Encouraged eVideos
New Online course

Would you be interested in helping encourage other men?
Yes

What kind of encouragement would you like to leave other men with in conclusion to what you've already shared?

Be strong the LORD is GREAT, He hears our prayers, HE will show HIS Face to whomever will seek HIM wholeheartedly. And that above all, if you let Him, nothing is impossible to HIM and lastly, we shouldn't be lukewarm Christians but men who know the Lord personally.

~ *Jean Luc in Mauritius*

Chapter 34

Sarah

"Then He gave to Abraham,
and restored his wife Sarah to him...
because of Sarah, Abraham's wife."
—Genesis 20:14, 18

Ministry Note: *This testimony is just shy of being long enough to be one of our Restoration Journey Novels, so the Lord led us to include it here to conclude this Testimony book.*

Prolog

To the Beloved of my soul I give all the glory, praise and worship. Thank You for Your presence in my life, for taking me through the narrow path. For bringing me sorrow and pain to get my attention and making me bow down at Your feet.

Jesus You are everything that I need! Thank You for supplying all my needs: spiritual, emotional, physical, and financial. You are amazing! Thank You for what I'm still waiting for that I know will come in Your time, not mine: Eating for Your glory and as a result, losing weight; getting a driving license; a car; having my marriage restored for Your glory; one day having children, "Thank You for our future children Sarah and Benjamin who already exist in Your heart and for the grace to be a worker at home and mother."

Thank You for this book You have written through my journey, and the testimony of our time spent together. May it be used for Your glory and praise and to help other women. Thank You, too, for the privilege to tithe to my storehouse RMIEW who have fed me your truths. Thank You for taking care of me and letting me be comforted in Your arms. I love You My Husband, My love.

~ Sarah

Chapter 1

My Restoration Journey Begins

Friday, October 26, 2012

This is the 1st time I've filled out a Marriage Evaluation Questionnaire. I speak Portuguese. I'm currently married and my husband lives with me. I've shared my situation with my husband's family. I've shared my situation with friends/neighbors. I've never read any of your books. My age is between 31-40. I have been married for 2 years. Yes, I want help but my husband doesn't. I've gained weight.

The biggest problem for Matt is because I am overweight. He met me this way, he never saw me slim before, because I've never been a slim woman. He said he liked big women before but on our honeymoon I was so big that he now is traumatized and doesn't fancy me anymore.

I met Jesus when I was 16, I was in an Assembly of God in Brazil. After that I went to another Pentecostal church and finally to a Baptist church. When I was 37 I ran away from the Lord, moved to Wales and started a life going out with many men. God used Matt to stop my life of ongoing fornication. When I was living with Matt, as a girlfriend, I started going back to church and seeking the Lord again.

Yes, I feel my situation is hopeless. If I look at the things with human eyes, it is hopeless but I know that God will make a way, I just don't know what to do anymore, how to cope, how to treat a husband who brings his affair and another woman to our home and is forcing me to leave. Should I leave?

Why do I want my Marriage Restored? First because I believe God didn't bring Matt in my life just for a romantic reason. He is the most complicated man I ever met and all of his life is a mess. I strongly believe God has a purpose in his life and wants to use him, his testimony to help other husbands in the same situation. I believe God made my marriage: everything was against me, and God made many miracles for us to be together. And even though he cheated with just one woman a month after our wedding, I know God hates divorce, and I hate it as well. I want to be a living testimony of what His word can do. And I believe He permitted it to bring me close to Him because my husband was an idol for me and I can only have one God in my life.

Why did I come? I am a Brazilian Christian since I was 16, but when I was 37 I moved to Wales and away from the Lord, lost my virginity, went out with many men until I met my husband, Matt, who is Irish.

We lived together as boyfriend and girlfriend for almost 2 years, and even then the Lord was already working in my life and showing me I was in fornication and I shouldn't live that way.

I started asking the Lord to touch Matt's heart to marry me so we could live according to God's way. When I started doing it God's way that is when the problems began. He cheated on me, started to humiliate me (I am overweight, he met me this way and I never been slim) and asked me to leave his house (I had moved to his house).

We spent one year apart and during this time I was asking God to do His will and if it was His plan for us to marry, to prepare everything. It was one of the most painful periods of my life. One day he invited me to come and we slept together, after that he just asked me to leave and said he was with someone else. From that day I made a vow with the Lord that I would never sleep with any man before being married. And God really separated us. Months without any contact.

Because I was living in Wales I needed a visa, I came from Brazil with a student visa which had to be renewed every year. The government made this process more and more difficult and that very year I couldn't do it anymore, I couldn't afford to have a part time job and pay for my university courses.

My heart was broken because I had to go back to Brazil and be away from the one I was praying for and asking for God to change our lives. The only person who knew about this was my best friend in Brazil, who all the time helped me with prayers.

One month before my student visa expired, Matt's mum had a surgery and he said I was the only one he could bring with him to visit his mum at the hospital, as I already met all of his family. One week after that, he invited me for a dinner to thank me for the support and at this dinner he put himself on his knees and said he went out with many women while we were apart, looking for something but none of them were like me. He said he didn't want me to go back to Brazil and asked me to be his wife. I just cried, that was what I was praying for, for the previous 3 years.

I just would like to say that all the time God was giving me words of affirmation and saying He would do a miracle. He said He took me out of the house as a prostitute and would bring me back legally, as a wife. It was very hard to carry on believing, especially because my time was running out to remain in Wales, but one day using someone preaching at church God said: "I will do a miracle, but it will happen at the very end."

In Wales, if you are not from the European Community, like me, you have to ask permission to get married, but I had to have at least 3 months in my visa for that. At the time I had less than one. Matt didn't believe they would allow us to marry but I carried on praying for a miracle, if that was God's will for us. He proposed on March 16th, my visa expired on April 30th and on May 18th the government sent me a letter saying we weren't allowed to marry because of the lack of time on my visa but they would make an *exception* and let us marry! They reminded me because we didn't ask for permission before I was already illegally here, but they gave a document in which I was allowed to marry up until August, but it didn't change my illegal immigration status.

We had to go to the register office and the final word would come from them, if they said no, I had to go back to Brazil. For that we had to arrange an interview and to show them we weren't a fake couple. We went and even with my expired visa in hand (that time, in May, I was already illegally living in Wales but legal to marry), the officer set up the date for our wedding. Soon after that, we were officially engaged and I made a vow to the Lord to never be with a man before marriage again. We didn't have any physical contact and we did not live together. One day while I was visiting at his house someone knocked on the door, a woman.

One more time I had to fight in prayers, the next day I asked him for a decision, he said he would marry me.

After that he changed for the better, he was really interested in preparing everything for our wedding, it was that time when we arranged all the details: it was a simple ceremony with just his family, some friends and my cousin (my only family here). It was the perfect day, full of love and God's presence.

After the wedding Matt started to change again.

One day I came back from work and we both got in bed and he carried on humiliating me and asked me to leave the house because it was his. We had been married for 2 years, but again the visa problem surfaced. When you marry with a UK citizen (Wales is part of the UK), we receive a 2-year spouse visa, after that we can apply for settlement in Wales, but we have to carry on as married for that amount of time. That is the only reason he still allowed me to live in our house. All my documents are with the Home Office (the government) and all this time, these 2 years I am continually praying for a change.

I didn't marry my husband for a visa, unfortunately I need it to live with him. I don't want a divorce, God hates divorce. I made all the mistakes a wife could make, confronted the woman and now the worse is that he is bringing her to our home, saying she's going to move in.

I believe only God can save my marriage, I cannot do it alone and I don't know what to do, how to pray anymore or how to cope. I don't want to leave my home, but if this is God's will to work in Matt's heart, if this is the only way, I will go. I just know that is what God is using to keep me here in this country, the fact that my settlement didn't arrive yet.

I never asked him to leave, I couldn't because it is his house. I know it is my house as well, but he doesn't recognize that. He is asking me to leave so *she* can move in.

I am sorry this is so long but I need God's guidance and help, I know He is the only One who can help me.

God bless you all.

—————Chapter 2 —————

Becoming a Marriage Minister: My BIO

Sunday, March 31, 2013

It's been just over five months and I am close to finishing my lessons on your site. Thank you! Today I was challenged to turn my vision to helping others and took the step to become a Marriage Minister.

The first assignment is to work with a team to build a BIO but due to the sensitive nature of my situation, RMI asked that I use a "Hidden Woman" name; often known as a pen name. Today is the day I became Sarah.

Oi, meu nome é Sarah, which translates to *Hi, my name is Sarah* in Portuguese, is how my BIO began, and I was able to share much of what I have already opened up about in the last chapter. Having opened up, I then continued by sharing how much more the Lord wanted to change me by bringing me through one crises and heartbreak after another.

During my engagement period and right after the wedding, my husband continued to be mean-spirited and disrespectful towards me. The sins of alcoholism and adultery continued to plague his life. He became involved with another woman, brought her to the house, and asked me to leave, again. It was a never ending nightmare.

I wanted my nightmare to end and that's when I came across the RMI website, at the end of October 2012, in the same year my spouse visa was due to expire and just after my husband asked me to leave. I began the courses RMI offered one month later. The courses opened my eyes to the truth laid out in the lessons and in God's word. Through the ministry's courses, the Lord made me see that I made my earthly husband and my marriage my gods, which is an abomination to our Heavenly Husband.

The Lord showed me how to be a gentle and quiet spirit through several trials and testing with my husband that I had to endure. For many days and nights, the OW slept over and I had to be quiet in our bedroom. Many times neighbors would come by to inform me that they saw the OW entering the house, and they were angry with my husband over it.

As my Saviour began transforming my life, the hate wall between me and my husband began to crumble. This was truly an act of God's grace and mercy. The Lord became my all and all. I just stood back and watched my Heavenly Husband fight these battles on my behalf and every time my husband asked me to leave, the next day he would say he wasn't ready for me to go and asked me to stay until I received the right to live permanently in Wales. I must confess that many times, I just wanted to run away because of all the humiliation. However, each time God would say to me, "My grace is enough for you; be still and know that I am God."

In December 2012 I was granted permanent residence in Wales. The time to leave my home had arrived. I waited so long for my permanent residency, but when I received the news I cried because I knew I had to go. To my surprise when my husband gave me my residence's card, he also cried. At that moment, I realized the Lord was really fighting for our marriage, and He would bring glory to His name because the battle belongs to Him.

The OW started to be bitter like the Word says. My husband asked me to stay until April 2013.

In April they broke up. I could see my restoration at the corner. But soon he found someone else and asked me to leave again. God was breaking me completely. In obedience I left my home in May 2013. The night before I left we spent it crying together. My husband expressed that he was very conflicted with his feelings towards me. I couldn't understand anything that was going on between us and the pain was almost unbearable.

I had so many battles to fight: my husband's adultery, my living situation, my spiritual adultery, my idolatry, and gluttony, which is my biggest enemy. At one point, I took up residency in the land of confusion and stopped doing my RMI courses, thus the reasons for much of my pain and suffering I ultimately went through. However, the Lord continued to be faithful to me. Every night that I was in pain, the Lord comforted me. I asked Him to use my pain to draw me closer to Him.

However, through God's love, my Saviour provided me with shelter through an affordable bedroom in a lady's flat, allowed me to complete my studies to get my diploma in social and health care (equivalent to high school diploma in America), and opened a door for a better job as a health care assistant. The Lord is still helping me to win the battle with my weight.

I don't know what the Lord has for me, but I'm learning day by day that there is no joy in life without Him, even if you have a husband, a home and children. If God is not there with you nothing can bring you joy or fulfill your life. Only when He is the first in your life you can experience real peace. There is no reason to exist without Him.

After understanding that I have to carry my own cross, God ministered His peace in my heart, which is what I want to pass along to other women. My trials have been so difficult that I can no longer receive nourishment from milk—I need solid food of God's presence and details of His Word. I believe that the Lord will use me one day to share my testimony in a book, just like *Erica Kramer - My Restoration Journey, A True Story Novel.* However, I still have many trials to overcome and lessons to be learned.

To be perfectly honest, I don't know what my life would had been like if God didn't bring me to this ministry. I thank the Lord for Erin, this ministry and my ePartner, for their encouragement and love for the Lord. They helped me to learn how to carry my cross and grow in Christ's love.

Ladies, do not leave your cross for someone else to carry. Do not take your eyes away from our Heavenly Husband. Love Him with all your understanding, strength, heart and soul, and as always…

BE ENCOURAGED!

Chapter 3

Spiritually Fed: My Lessons Begin

November 12, 2012

Today I read my first lesson and filled out the form to journal and document what I am learning. In the lesson I began learning the power of the word of God—that it can heal me immediately! It can bring me comfort and when I am in pain God uses it to touch me and to give me grace to carry on.

I keep repeating everything again and again, all the verses that I know because God is using them to heal me. Excitedly, I will learn more everyday.

Before meditating on His word, I used to let my thoughts dominate me: fear, worry, anger and sorrow would overwhelm me. Now I confess the word instead. I am still fighting and crying a lot, but I know one day God will heal my heart completely.

I feel God closer to me. He gave me Isaiah 54, I didn't know what was written there and when I read it I cried. The Lord was speaking to me, to me, a sinner, a woman who destroyed her husband's love. The Lord was telling me He will never leave me, He is my Husband.

Thank You Lord.

Also, today, I realized I have sinned so much; every day God is reminding me of something that I have done or said that hurt my husband so that I can confess this to my Lord and Husband, asking for His grace to continue to change me.

Just yesterday, for example, I went to the family planning clinic to get contraceptives; I received for the whole year. Before my marriage, I had problems with my period, it was very heavy and painful so I started to take the combined pills and my period stopped. Actually, it was a relief. But around 2 months ago my husband asked me to stop taking contraceptives and at that point even though he was with the OW, and we were not having any kind of intimacy, I didn't stop. He even said he believed that was one of the reasons I was overweight due to taking them. But because of the problems with my period, I didn't *want* to stop, so I told him that and I carried on taking the pills. This means I didn't submit to my husband or to God.

Even while waiting for the appointment, the Holy Spirit reminded me that my husband asked me to stop and God started telling me to obey him.

I confess it is not easy for me, but I understand that God is giving me an opportunity to do the right thing and I will do it, in Jesus' name, and because of this—my period now is in God's hands.

This makes me very happy because the Lord is giving me directions as my heart is to want to do His will.

The main thing that I learned today was to find out that I *was* in sin and not only my husband. It was I who had destroyed my marriage with my wrongdoing and I was totally blind and never could see it. I have made all the mistakes in the book: I confronted him and the OW; didn't submit to him; called him to say I loved him; bought flowers for him; and it proved I was like a dog seeking attention—that is why he called me chewing gum. This lesson was really worthy my time and opened my eyes!!!

Not only sin and why I was treated badly, but I also discovered I am not alone. God had permitted all this in my life to change my heart, bring me close to Him, save my husband and restore our marriage. I had to pass through it. My testimony will be unique and to God's glory.

I just want to be faithful to the One who called us as a couple to share with the world this great miracle that I believe already has started to happen.

To You my Lord, Lover of my soul, be all the glory and honor and praise forever. Teach me to love You more than anything; to love Your presence and to leave everything behind so that I can be one with You.

Teach me to obey Your word, unconditionally.

Holy Spirit I need You more and more. I need to hear Your voice and follow Your advice. To learn how to treat my husband and not respond in the flesh every time. You gave us an opportunity to be together. Jesus, Son of the living God, You are my Husband. Take my hand and let me see You as my Groom.

Thank You Lord for this first day of lessons. I love You.

Before I end, I have to say that the testimony today encouraged me. My minister also sent me a testimony through a wonderful book that I read, all the 179 pages in one day, *Erica Kramer*. Amazingly, it was my only day off during the week. I just could feel her pain and visualize everything she wrote. It gave me courage and comforted my heart. The way God worked in this couples lives touched me. God is the same, He is the same powerful God who worked in their lives, and therefore, He will do the same in our lives too.

The similarities were Erica's husband's coldness; but how God allowed her to be in the fiery furnace (like I am now); how she describes the many times when she failed and the mercy of the Lord was with her; how God supplied all her necessities, spiritual, emotional and material. The Lord always had a word for Erica and ministered to her personally— taking her to the Bible and showing her how she had done things wrong in the past but how she could obey Him now, giving her the opportunity to fix things through His grace.

What Erica used to change was the word of God, repentance, humility, and learning how to hear and obey the Holy Spirit's voice. Now that is my goal too.

Be Encouraged!

———Chapter 4 ———

Reflecting on my Journey

Sunday, January 19, 2014

"Unless the Lord builds a house, the work of the builders is wasted. Unless the Lord protects a city, guarding it with sentries will do no good." Psalm 127:1

All the glory, honour and praise belongs to the Almighty God, who is with us all the time!

As we are approaching the end of 2013, and wow, what a year. I am reflecting on what the Lord has done in me and for me during my journey with Him, which started October 2012. It's so amazing how the Lord uses everything, He wants to talk to us, to open our eyes and to teach us His way. God really doesn't waste anything!

When I got married 3 years ago, the engagement ring that was given to me was a second hand one. At the time it broke my heart, I never had heard about a bride who had a second hand engagement ring! It is an 18ct gold ring with a tiny little diamond. Pretty, yes, but it's second hand! There was nothing I could do but wait and hope that one day my earthly husband "earthly husband " would "repent" and give me a new ring that "I truly deserved." (I never said a word, but desired it in my heart.)

Then about 2 years later, I noticed something was wrong with the ring and as I kept looking at it from time to time, one day I saw the diamond was loose! Four prongs were broken (prongs are the little metal claws that bend over the edge of the diamond to hold it securely in place, there were 8 on my ring). I was devastated! With all that was going on in my home and me being a contentious wife, the last thing my husband would care about was a broken, second hand engagement ring so I put it in a safe place and bought a silver one similar to mine. Then I bought another one, and another one and another one. I have around six fake engagement rings, but I missed my ring and wanted it restored. More than that, I wanted a new one!

The journey for the restoration of my marriage with the Lord started and as He was dealing with me, He showed that He was more important than any ring because, "Wherever your treasure is, there the desires of your heart will also be." Luke 12:34

The Lord has been blessing me more than I would ever imagine with His presence, care and love. While I'm living away from home, He is revealing Himself as my Heavenly Husband and supplying all my needs.

Recently I took a look at the ring again and felt the desire to have it restored because it is a jewel and I didn't mind anymore that it was second hand or if one day I would have a new one. Nothing happens in vain and that was the ring the Lord gave me. "And we know that in all things God works for the good of those who love Him, who have been called according to His purpose." Romans 8:28

Then I prayed: Lord if that is Your will, guide me to the place where it can be restored for a price I can afford. I've been in many places but wasn't sure in my heart until I found one shop which I could divide the payment in 6 months that I could really afford. I left the ring there and two weeks later I had a phone call saying:

"When the jeweller started repairing your ring he found out that not only the 4 prongs were broken but the ring's base (head) was also broken and he cannot repair it unless the base is completely repaired first! So, to repair the base will be much more expensive and take a longer time, are you willing to do that or would you like your ring back without any repairs?"

It was such a surprise that I couldn't give any answer straight away and asked for some time to think (pray). I prayed and asked for the Lord's guidance. I knew He had guided me to that shop so why was all of this happening now? If He took me there, with a price I could afford, why would it be much more expensive to have it repaired now?

After some days I didn't have a direct word but I felt peace in my heart to have the ring restored because The Lord is my shepherd; I have all that I need. And this same God who takes care of me will supply all my needs from His glorious riches, which have been given to us in Christ Jesus. Psalm 23:1, Philippians 4:19

So I said "yes" to the jeweller!

Days later, I was sharing what the Lord is doing in my life with my ePartner and I told her about the ring, she also shared all the good the Lord is doing in her life. It was so nice to have the Lord in the middle of us when we were praising Him for taking care of us so well and while she was talking something clicked in my heart!!! The ring! The Lord is talking to us through the ring!

I knew the ring needed to be restored and I thought it was something superficial. I compromised myself to pay for it but when the jeweller started his work, he realized the base needed to be completely restored otherwise nothing could be done, the ring would never be repaired! While my e-partner was still talking I started to cry and told her what came to my heart. I didn't have to explain anything because the Holy Spirit was also talking to her and showing her the parallel between the ring and the restoration of our marriage with the Lord, and willing Him, our earthly husband   s. Then she started to cry and we both agreed I should write a Praise Report about it.

Now I understand better why the Lord took me away from my home and I am now living in a rented room. He has started "to repair." He is the Potter and we are the clay:

"The Lord gave another message to Jeremiah. He said, 'Go down to the potter's shop, and I will speak to you there.' So I did as he told me and found the potter working at his wheel. But the jar he was making did not turn out as he had hoped, so he crushed it into a lump of clay again and started over. Then the Lord gave me this message: 'O Israel, can I not do to you as this potter has done to his clay? As the clay is in the potter's hand, so are you in my hand.'" Jeremiah 18:1-6

Are you willing to wait? Are you willing to give "your ring" in the hands of the Heavenly Jeweller so He can repair not only the broken parts of your ring you can see but repair all the base which is damaged? Are you willing to give your heart and what is precious to you in the hands of the Heavenly Jeweller?

"Anyone who listens to my teaching and follows it is wise, like a person who builds a house on solid rock. Though the rain comes in torrents and the flood waters rise and the winds beat against that house, it won't collapse because it is built on bedrock. But anyone who hears my teaching and doesn't obey it is foolish, like a person who builds a house on sand. When the rains and floods come and the winds beat against that house, it will collapse with a mighty crash." Matthew 7:24-27

The shop promised my ring would be repaired in 2 weeks and I would have it back before Christmas. Today is the 29th of December and I still haven't received it back. They apologized and said the jeweller is working on it but the damage is really big. I left the shop with a smile on my face (I don't think they understood why), but I was happy!

It doesn't matter how long it will take anymore! I know the ring is in safe hands, and in His time, which is perfect, He will give it back to me. When I look to the ring on my finger I will remember no more about a second hand engagement ring but that the Lord, the Heavenly Jeweller, broke it completely to make it new and this ring will be like a memorial of His unfailing love towards me and not just about my marriage anymore. This ring will remind me about the restoration of my marriage with Him, my Lord, my Heavenly Husband!

O beloved, can I not do to you as this jeweller has done to this ring?

Be encouraged!

Chapter 5

"A Foolish Woman"

Monday, January 6, 2014

"In the same way, you wives must accept the authority of your husbands. Then, even if some refuse to obey the Good News, your godly lives will speak to them without any words. They will be won over. For instance, Sarah obeyed her husband, Abraham, and called him her master. You are her daughters when you do what is right without fear of what your husbands might do." 1 Peter 3:1,6 (NLT)

I have been living in the Wales for 8 years, the Lord brought me here, to the desert, to bless me and turn me into His beloved bride. The road has been arduous. Like most of you, I experienced pain, tears, humiliations but most of all I have seen the hand of the Almighty God, who reveals Himself as "The Faithful Husband", as the One who takes care of every detail in my life. To Him all glory and power forever!

In my home country, Brazil, and around the world the Lord has revealed Himself as comforter, strong tower, protector, best friend to so many women like me who came to RMIEW. Women have experienced God's hands taking away the pain of discovering themselves betrayed and opening the eyes of their understanding, showing them that "A wise woman builds her home, but a foolish woman...a foolish woman tears it down with her own hands." And so we find we were all foolish, full of pride, feeling wronged or unjustly treated but the truth is, we were and many of us still are, rebellious and unsubmissive.

Today, reading my lesson about submission, I read that Abraham's wife Sarah was obedient to a husband who lied and deceived because he was afraid to die. Have you ever thought about Sarah's feelings when she had to say Abraham was her brother and ended up in Pharaoh's harem? (Genesis 12)

But she did not even open her mouth, she didn't argue or say: "Are you out of your mind, are you going to give your wife to another man? I'm not doing this because this is not God's will! Abraham you are wrong! ... bla bla bla ... "

No! We cannot hear Sarah's voice, because she didn't even open her mouth! But that's why the Lord noted her submission and mentioned her in the New Testament as an example of a submissive and obedient wife:

"In the same way, you wives must accept the authority of your husbands. Then, even if some refuse to obey the Good News, your godly lives will speak to them without any words. They will be won over. For

instance, Sarah obeyed her husband, Abraham, and called him her master. You are her daughters when you do what is right without fear of what your husbands might do." 1 Peter 3:1,6 (NLT)

Have you noticed it says: "without fear of what your husbands might do"?

The Greek word for fear is φοβέω (phobeō), which means to be afraid, to be struck with fear, to be seized with alarm, to flee!

Why am I sharing all this?

Because I have been separated for 7 months. I had to leave the house which was one of the most painful moments of my life, but now I know that it wasn't my earthly husband who took me out of my home but my Heavenly Husband, to deal with me in a deeper way. By God's mercy the hate wall doesn't exist anymore and the Lord has been allowing me to go back home once or twice a week. Unfortunately, alcohol and cigarettes have been present in my home- I loathe them! Almost every time I'm home I am asked by my earthly husband to buy them. Before this journey with the Lord I argued and was extremely contentious, called him a drunk, said I would not feed his addictions...bla bla bla.

Then the Lord began ministering to me and telling me to go and buy what he asked for *without saying a word,* but boy, how much it hurt and still hurts. Many times I leave the house crying and come back with a drink and a pack of cigarettes telling the Lord how much I hate all these and asking Him to deliver me. As a Christian it is a humiliation for me even to carry these things.

I must confess, before this journey I couldn't understand why Sarah didn't protest when she was taken to Pharaoh's harem. Today I understand that the Lord allows pain and humiliations in our lives for a purpose, to trigger something. There is no honor without humiliation. To be healed you need to go through the pain. God never wastes a pain, or a humiliation.

Back to my lesson, what I mean is that the Lord sees that I only go out to buy alcohol and cigarettes for the sake of obedience. Obedience to my earthly husband ? No, my obedience is obedience to God who tells me to do what he asks: "without fear of what your husbands might do"!

I know one day the Lord will use every single day that I went to buy these things and came back crying, to bring glory to His name. I already can see that because so often my husband tells me he knows that I have no obligation to purchase these things and how much he appreciates the fact I am doing it for him. We also must not forget that the Lord is also working in our husband's hearts and writing their testimonies—not just our testimonies. Everything that happens to them now will be understood by them (and others) later—each will look back and will see the Lord!

"But to those called by God to salvation, both Jews and Gentiles, Christ is the power of God and the wisdom of God. This foolish plan of God is wiser than the wisest of human plans, and God's weakness is stronger than the greatest of human strength." 1 Corinthians 1:24

Beloved your obedience and submission will bring glory to the name of the Lord, He never slumbers or sleeps, He is never late! He will defend you, deliver you, set your heart free so you will be completely His!

Do not forget to always confess:

"But as for me and my family, we will serve the Lord." Joshua 24:15

Be encouraged!

——— Chapter 6 ———

Not Afraid to Speak Out

"I have told all your people about your justice. I have not been afraid to speak out, as you, O Lord, well know. I have not kept the good news of Your justice hidden in my heart; I have talked about Your faithfulness and saving power."

"Now all glory to God, who is able, through His mighty power at work within us, to accomplish infinitely more than we might ask or think. Glory to Him in the church and in Christ Jesus through all generations forever and ever! Amen." Ephesians 3:20-21

Today I was reading Psalms and the Lord spoke to me, to be honest with you. He reminded me of a principle that I wasn't obeying: to open my mouth and tell others about His marvelous works in my life.

Psalm 40: 9-10a says: "I have told all your people about your justice. I have not been afraid to speak out, as you, O Lord, well know. I have not kept the good news of Your justice hidden in my heart; I have talked about Your faithfulness and saving power."

The Holy Spirit said: "You are not sharing what I've done and what I am doing in your life!"

Then verse 10: "I have told everyone in the great assembly of Your unfailing love and faithfulness."

Since I'm not going to church anymore once I started with this ministry in October 2012, each of you are the great assembly! Ladies, we are one in Christ and we are His church, we minister to each other every day and we eat His Word and principles from God's hands.

So by God's grace, from today on, I don't want to keep for myself what the Lord is doing in my life anymore and I ask your forgiveness for being selfish and lazy to share it all with you. Failing to share it means

I have delayed my progress with the Lord while denying you the opportunity to also give Him all the glory that He deserves.

God is working and breaking me on a daily basis and He's been more than amazing to me.

As you know, I'm married but separated. I went through a very painful process because after walking with this ministry and being blessed, broken, seeing the changes in my relationship with my earthly husband and after all the grace the Lord gave me because the current OW slept over in our home for months, I just couldn't understand. When I believed I was going to be restored, my husband, instead asked me to move out. Today, 5 months later I'm still living in a rented bedroom, with no hate wall between us, but I'm just a friend of my husband, not a wife.

So as I wrote before, I want to start to share all the good the Lord is doing in my life since I had to move out of my home. We don't have children and I praise the Lord for that since it would be much harder if we had children, although I believe one day they will come and I already pray for them. I'm 41 and every circumstance says this is impossible, but if it is God's will for them to be born who will stop Him???

The first blessing was concerning finding a place to live. I live in the Wales, but I'm from Brazil, I've been living here for 8 years now. So to me, it's very expensive to rent a flat or house in Wales, so I was only able to rent a bedroom. I asked the Lord to guide me to a place where I didn't have to share with any man—thankfully, He heard my prayer and guided me to a bedroom closer to where I work and also close to my home. There is just one lady living there. I also asked Him for a double bed (the rooms here are classified as *single* if they have a single bed or double if they have a double bed, which are more expensive than the singles). Not surprisingly, the Lord provided a double bedroom with a price of a single bedroom!!! He's always faithful to His brides!

I admit it was extremely painful to leave my home, my things, my duties as a wife, but, looking back the Lord prepared everything ahead of time. So this means I can easily believe this is for my good (as I realized after I left that I am comforted), because He has everything in control.

The last blessing of this report is that as soon as I moved in I received a check with a tax refund! In the 8 years I've been living in Wales, I never ever received any tax refund—for the glory of His name— the amount was exactly the same that I had to pay for my monthly rent! I just dropped to my knees and cried knowing that no matter what was happening to me and even in the middle of all confusion and sadness because I had to leave my home, He was saying He was here with me and He, as my Husband, would provide and take care of me.

For now I can be His bride, not a wife, and I also no longer am in the next room when my earthly husband shares his bed with an OW—what could be better?

So my dear sister and friend, the Lord loves you, He takes care of you and He will never leave or forsake you. In the middle of your pain just close your eyes and know that He is Your Husband.

Because I am bringing my tithe to my storehouse, this ministry, I've seen the Lord be more than faithful to me. I have all that I need, which is Him.

Very soon I will share many more blessings! Be encouraged!

——Chapter 7 ——

Darkest before the Light

Wednesday, April 18, 2013

"Yea though I walk through the valley of the shadow of death, I will fear no evil, for Thou art with me." Psalm 23:4 KJV

It's more than interesting that this is the seventh chapters, indication "it is finished" because soon after I submitted this chapter for publication, my Restoration Journey Novel stopped.

All the glory, honor, praise and worship to You Beloved of my soul, Jesus Christ. My dear Lord, only You know how hard this month was! During all this journey I'm sure this was one of the hardest ones, there were moments I really thought I was going to die but You were there, once again, like always! My heart is so heavy Lord and I just hope You will break it completely one day. I thank You because I am not restored yet, I cannot!

You have to be the first and You are still working in me. I could see Your faithfulness in the middle of my rebellion and I cannot explain how amazing Your mercy is. Thank You for everything You have done for me this month, all the blessings: my husband's passport, the Brazilian Consulate appointment, the holidays to Brazil, spending Easter at home. Thank You for looking after me while I was so ill, everything came at once but You were here. This holidays will be our first together Lord and I ask You to work on me. My husband and home are in Your hands, let Your will be done... The book is on Lord and the devil is fuming but the victory is Yours!!! You brought me until here... My life is in Your hands, I love You. Sarah

Monday, May 18, 2014

My dear Sarah,

I'm relieved to know you are home and the Lord has taken you away to be on a honeymoon with Him. I know most of what this book has been about and its focus, was written a long time ago. But when I read it, I still felt like I was kicked in the gut because of the severity of your pain and your suffering. Because all of it is due to only one thing—that you still see you earthly husband as your husband, and you haven't yet experienced the Lord as your Husband. And because you do, you don't realize being removed from your home was "for your good" but feel it is some sort of punishment. Once you understand it was to bless you, you will begin to heal and finally rejoice with overflowing joy because you and your Beloved Husband are finally alone and together! Sorrow and struggles will be turned into joy and a sense of freedom.

Maybe the change is already happening there in Brazil, but just to be sure I am sending you our new Heavenly Husband chapter to give you something to think about. My concern is that instead of showing the women reading your book how to be free from pain, by finding their heavenly Husband, you instead are trying to make them accept their situation, by enduring their suffering with an unfaithful husband. When instead, it's about finding a new and faithful, loving Husband.

Personally, I've had trouble continuing to read about someone who is always suffering, and each time hope and expect to read more than just despair and horror. We, the readers and I, need to see relief happening soon, and that's only going to happen if you let go of your earthly husband and seeing yourself as his wife and instead, and then see yourself as the Lord's bride.

As I said, I'm hoping that being in Brazil will finally allow you to begin to focus on your heavenly Husband who, I believe, took you there for a honeymoon with Him. My hope is that you're not lamenting about her earthly husband any more because I don't think we can move forward with your Restoration Journey Novel if things don't change.

Instead of encouraging women about their heavenly Husband you are instead showing them how to remain a wife, despite the pain, and with a man who wants more than one wife. As horrible as it is to be rejected and left for an OW, being one of many "wives" is worse, like when you were sleeping in the next room to them and cleaning up after them both.

There's no question this is horrible and far more difficult than what most women are being asked to endure. But as the end times approach, sin is worsening and we are already seeing more and more women who are willing to share and be intimate with their husband who is treating more than one woman as a wife.

This book and our ministry cannot promote "acceptance" which the bible does warn us will come. Even the standers ministries who sadly encourage sleeping with an ex-husband is obscuring the truth. If a woman is still legally married, yes, we need to continue to remain intimate, but not because we need love from him, but because of His love for us. You understand that we simply can't promote what you once were asked to do and be—but He has already delivered you from it—in order for you to be His bride. First by moving you out of your husband's home, and now sending you far across the globe. Even though you've completed all six months of courses, you are still spiritually where our beginners RYM Course 1 students are *"I am not restored yet"* By the time women begin Rebuilding, most are, instead, enjoying their relationship with their heavenly Husband, and most don't even want their marriage restored (which of course is when restoration always happens).

Sarah, as difficult it is to have to say this, but if you are unwilling to let go of your earthly husband so you can begin to see the Lord as your Husband (which we will immediately see in your praise reports), then we have to shelf the idea of continuing to promote and work on your Restoration Journey Novel.

Though this may seem harsh, we hope it will instead motivate you to see what He wants for you AND how He wants to use **you** to help women out of where you've been locked up for far too long: in the dungeon of despair due to who you still long for, your husband and restoration, rather than who wants to be your Husband when you then will fully be restored! Psalm 23 "He restores my soul..."

Just as you want to your earthly husband to let go of each of the OW he's been involved with, so that you would be his *only* "wife" so too your heavenly Husband wants you to be HIS alone!

Please write again when you can to let me know of your breakthrough and describe your Honeymoon in Brazil *with your loving Husband.*

That's when we will rejoice with you!!

~ Erin

Sarah: Amen Erin, what you wrote it's the truth and I agree with you to stop my Restoration Journey to experience becoming His bride. I will remain here, alone, with the Lord.

Thankfully, the Lord proved that even in death there is resurrection and soon after my mandatory time off from writing my book and doing any more lessons, I experienced the LORD in a way I never dreamed I would! Gone was the pain, and Erin was so right. Soon after the letter she wrote me while I was in Brazil, the time I spent there—He was with me all the time!!

When the time came to leave, I didn't want to return to Wales and I couldn't stop crying. But then He said, "You are not returning to that bedroom or that situation, you are returning to be with Me" and suddenly I felt His grace all over me, which enabled me to return back home to be with Him there. All I know is that He loves me so much and I'm asking Him to conquer my heart and once and for all to be His bride fully. I would say I'm still in the process, but now I know there's nothing better in this life than the Lord!

Be Encouraged!

————Chapter 8 ————

I Finally Found Him

Thursday, June 28, 2014

Much time has past since my last chapter, due to a mandatory time off from ministering that I already mentioned. And as I said, during that time off everything changed in me and so did my writing. Instead of writing about my pain, without any effort, the pain was replaced by a spirit of gratitude brought on solely by Who I found. Here is a praise report I recently wrote.

"Better Than Ten Sons"

And Elkanah, her husband, said to her, "Hannah, why do you weep? And why do you not eat? And why is your heart sad? Am I not more to you than ten sons?" I Samuel 1:8

I just have finished a lesson entitled "Your Mother's Teachings" and I want to praise the Lord for His love towards me!!

It was not easy for me to start reading this lesson as I don't have children yet, but I was so grateful at the end because there is so much knowledge and wisdom shared!

Being a mum is a full time job and one that I dream about, at the same time I praise the Lord that it didn't happen yet—so He still can prepare me in a deeper way to be the mum He is calling me to be. It wasn't always like this and many times I suffered a lot for not being a mum at my age, but now I know that my Heavenly Husband has the control of everything and He is better than 10 sons (children), husband or home. So if the Lord asks me the same question that Elkanah asked Hannah my answer will be: Yes, You are!!!

If you still are without children, join me in this prayer:

Lord, I will be happy if You give me children, but now I am happy because You still haven't given me them. You are all I want, You are all I need, You are all I long for. Thank You Jesus.

"To Him who sits on the throne and to the Lamb be blessing and honor and glory and might forever and ever!" Revelation 5:13

"Every Good Gift Comes from Him"

"Likewise, wives, be subject to your own husbands, so that even if some do not obey the word, they may be won without a word by the conduct of their wives." 1 Peter 3:1

All the glory belongs to the Lord. With this Praise Report I just want to thank Him for this principle. I have been praised in some many ways that was beyond my imagination. My Heavenly Husband is responsible for that because the grace to obey His word comes from Himself.

I am naturally a slow learner, unfortunately, so the same has been happening about applying God's principles in my life but one thing He opened my eyes about was that:

"Every good gift and every perfect gift is from above, coming down from the Father of lights with whom there is no variation or shadow due to change." James 1:17

I never truly understood before that if something good happened to me it was actually from my Heavenly Husband. I was grateful but I didn't realise that it was coming from a Husband but thought it was coming from God as a Father, Friend, Comforter.

Now I understand! It comes from my Husband! My Husband!!!!!

This is amazing and I can see clearly how He cares for me and He loves me! He takes care of every single detail!

Today I was taken for a lunch out, but I knew in my heart my Heavenly Husband who was taking me out for lunch and it made me so happy. It also helped me to take my eyes away from my circumstances and put them back on the Lord.

Thank You for this principle Beloved of my soul. I love you!

Be encouraged!

———Chapter 9 ———

"Bring Your Tithe and also Your Heart"

June 28, 2014

"Bring the full tithe into the storehouse, that there may be food in my house. And thereby put me to the test, says the Lord of hosts, if I will not open the windows of heaven for you and pour down for you a blessing until there is no more need. I will rebuke the devourer for you, so that it will not destroy the fruits of your soil, and your vine in the field shall not fail to bear, says the Lord of hosts. Then all nations will call you blessed, for you will be a land of delight, says the Lord of hosts." Malachi 3:10-12

In May 2013 the Lord took me out of my home to protect me, to deliver me and to take care of me in a deeper way. I couldn't understand at the time but in His mercy He is showing me day by day His grace, love and tenderness.

Since I started bringing my tithe to my storehouse, He has supplied all my needs. I don't *need* anything, of course I haven't got a car or a driving license yet, but they will come in His time and according to His will. Actually I have more than I need: a cozy bedroom, clothes, shoes, a 40" smart TV to watch my Christian videos, a bicycle that takes me to work, also food, a laptop, and now He is giving me books. Then this week He gave me my first study Bible! If I need to take a bus, train or taxi— He pays the fares. He even took me to Brazil for a month and while there, He used my mum to pay for all my expenses!

So in May last year He was my Lord, now, one year later, He is my Husband.

"Fear not, for you will not be ashamed; Be not confounded, For you will not be disgraced; for you will forget the shame of your youth, and the reproach of your widowhood you will remember no more. For your

Maker is your Husband, the Lord of hosts is His name; and the Holy One of Israel is your Redeemer, the God of the whole earth He is called.

For the Lord has called you like a wife deserted and grieved in spirit, like a wife of youth when she is cast off, says your God. For a brief moment I deserted you, but with great compassion I will gather you. In overflowing anger for a moment I hid my face from you, but with everlasting love I will have compassion on you," says the Lord, your Redeemer." Isaiah 54:4-8

The verses above have been giving strength to each one of us and it doesn't matter your situation, He is faithful. I have been like Gomer, Hosea's wife towards the Lord. I have betrayed Him in so many ways but He never ever gives up on me and now He is turning my heart towards Him because:

"Therefore I will hedge up her way with thorns, and I will build a wall against her, so that she cannot find her paths. She shall pursue her lovers but not overtake them, and she shall seek them but shall not find them. Then she shall say, 'I will go and return to my first husband, for it was better for me then than now." Hosea 2:6-7

So with this Praise Report I just want to thank my Lord for His faithfulness, for accomplishing His promises left in Malachi 3 and Hosea 2, and I want to encourage you to bring your tithe but also your heart to His altar.

Be Encouraged!

———— Chapter 10 ————

My Journey Home: A New Chapter

"Husband says 'I Need You!'"

The troubles in my life began when I turned my heart away from the Lord. I put my earthly husband first in my life and was also a contentious wife. Although my earthly husband met me being overweight and loved me this way, he started to say I was too big for him. And as a result he began committing adultery and bringing other women into our home. At this point, the Lord had my full attention.

My Beloved brought me through many trials to break me and mold me into His image. Through these trials, he showed me His love and faithfulness. He even took me away from my home to be alone with me, to heal me of my heartache, and to teach me His principles from His Word. But the most important reason He removed me from my home (when my husband told me to leave) was so He would show me that He was my Heavenly Husband.

During my trials, the Lord taught me how to keep silent and that I should run to Him and no one else with all my problems and questions. He showed me how to be quiet in His presence, to spend more and more time with Him and in His word. My heavenly Husband showed me how to let my earthly husband take the lead, and the importance of keeping relationships with like-minded women.

The Restoration Journey lessons offered by Encouraging Women helped me to get through the more difficult times when my earthly husband would bring the many different OWs to sleep over in our house. During this time, before He lovingly allowed me to move out, I had to be in the next bedroom, which was the hardest thing I had to do, but my heavenly Husband helped me through it. Through each encounter, my heavenly Husband was becoming my all in all.

The turning point of my restoration was when the Lord opened my eyes and showed me that there was no-one better than Him - not home, husband or children - all of these things had become idols to me. "For on account of a harlot one is reduced to a loaf of bread" (Psalm 6:26

NASB) which is what happened to my earthly husband when the Lord took away his job - which was a major turning point of my restoration.

1 Corinthians 2 (NLT) says "When I first came to you, dear brothers and sisters, I didn't use lofty words and impressive wisdom to tell you God's secret plan. For I decided that while I was with you I would forget everything except Jesus Christ, the One who was crucified. I came to you in weakness—timid and trembling. And my message and my preaching were very plain. Rather than using clever and persuasive speeches, I relied only on the power of the Holy Spirit. I did this so you would trust not in human wisdom but in the power of God.

"Yet when I am among mature believers, I do speak with words of wisdom, but not the kind of wisdom that belongs to this world or to the rulers of this world, who are soon forgotten. No, the wisdom we speak of is the mystery of God-His plan that was previously hidden, even though He made it for our ultimate glory before the world began. But the rulers of this world have not understood it; if they had, they would not have crucified our glorious Lord. That is what the Scriptures mean when they say, 'No eye has seen, no ear has heard, and no mind has imagined what God has prepared for those who love Him.' But it was to us that God revealed these things by His Spirit. For His Spirit searches out everything and shows us God's deep secrets. No one can know a person's thoughts except that person's own spirit, and no one can know God's thoughts except God's own Spirit.

"And we have received God's Spirit (not the world's spirit), so we can know the wonderful things God has freely given us. When we tell you these things, we do not use words that come from human wisdom. Instead, we speak words given to us by the Spirit, using the Spirit's words to explain spiritual truths. But people who aren't spiritual can't receive these truths from God's Spirit. It all sounds foolish to them and they can't understand it, for only those who are spiritual can understand what the Spirit means. Those who are spiritual can evaluate all things, but they themselves cannot be evaluated by others. For, 'Who can know the Lord's thoughts? Who knows enough to teach him?' But we understand these things, for we have the mind of Christ."

Once I truly found Him as my Heavenly Husband and experienced Him the way He wanted, it was finally my time to write my Restored Marriage Testimony. Yes, my restoration had finally arrived!

His time is always perfect and we all know it! Yet it is not until we let go of everything and then become His, only then are we truly ready.

Today I'm at home, precisely in the conservatory (sunroom or solarium in some countries). It's a beautiful sunny day and I'm surrounded by His peace and love. We all know the sentence: "There's no place like home" but the truth is "There is no place like being in the presence of the Lord!" I only can experience this peace because of Him as in this same place not long ago I experienced the worse days of my life. So I can say without reservations that we truly can trust Him when He says: "But where sin abounded, grace abounded much more, so that as sin reigned in death, even so grace might reign through righteousness to eternal life through Jesus Christ our Lord." Romans 5:20

My Lord reigns! Even though some circumstances haven't changed yet, even though there's an enemy still prowling around me like a roaring lion, even through everything— My Lord reigns! My God reigns! My Redeemer reigns! My Heavenly Husband reigns! And He has control of everything in His mighty hands!!! He is the Almighty God, the King of kings and the Lord of lords and nothing is impossible to Him!

All the glory, honour, praise and worship to the Lord of hosts, Author and Finisher of our faith, my Heavenly Husband!

Beginning today, my Heavenly Husband is writing a new chapter in my journey.

After 1 year and 2 months of living in a rented bedroom, alone with Him, He is revealing Himself to me, even more, in a lovely way, as I write my Restored Marriage Testimony.

"Jesus answered him, 'What I am doing you do not understand now, but afterwards you will understand'" (John 12:7)

As some of you know through "Sarah Edward: My Restoration Journey True Story Novel" it was hard for me to leave my home behind and at that time I couldn't understand why the Lord had allowed it to happen. For months I struggled, still desiring to return home, missing my things, while letting the sorrow and pain dominate my thoughts and heart. I was blind at all the Lord was doing in my life. But in the middle of all this He never let me down. He always gave comfort, He always had a song to sing and bring with it His healing.

When a man is in love with a woman he does everything for her. He is nice, kind, gentle but also firm at times in order to protect her from evil. Slowly he conquers her heart with his attention, his sweet voice, holding her hands and being there for her all the time. He covers her with gifts, flowers and jewelry. Ladies this is what the Lord has done with me!

"I have loved you, my people, with an everlasting love. With unfailing love I have drawn you to myself" (Jeremiah 31:3).

My healing came when the Lord took me on a vacation trip (called a holiday in the UK). He prepared everything so I could spend time with my mum and relatives in Brazil. Then, He touched my mums heart and she paid for everything!

But before my trip I still *longed* for my home and marriage restoration...that's when He started to admonish me about it...

Convicted, I realized I had been ungrateful, I was listening to the accuser, thinking I was being punished by my Lord when He took me away from home but instead of this, He took me away to protect me, deliver me and to be alone with me in order to conquer my heart! I really couldn't see it at the time but now I can—I can see it so clearly! This is love ladies! He let me feel sorrow in order to heal me! He let me cry to wipe my tears! He took everything away so I could finally see Him!

I am learning that the Lord has His own pace and time to work on us and nothing is automatic. When my journey began here with RMI I really couldn't see me in love with the Lord or living with Him as my Husband like so many of the women I read about were already living. Yes, I loved the Lord as my God, Father, Provider, Comforter but not as my Husband. I knew He had to be my all in all, but I just couldn't get there! At some point I thought I would never have a deeper relationship with Him.

Now I know this is His job, not ours. God wants to mould us to be Jesus' brides. So He took me away to allow Him to conquer my heart and to reveal Himself to me. He was doing it on a daily basis, using whatever He needed to break me and turn my heart towards Him. Day after day, He was patiently covering me with His wings, flooding me with His love!

So if you are where I used to be, not knowing how to love the Lord as your Heavenly Husband, just trust Him, just rest in His promises and He will do the rest. He will do everything He needs to conquer your heart; He is already doing it because you're here and reading this book!

My time away, my time in Brazil was amazing; He took care of every single detail. There I could hear His voice and see clearly how much He loves me and takes care of me. There, away from Wales, I could understand just how I needed just Him and life has no meaning if He is not in it as He longs to be.

Then when He had my heart He decided to take me back home. But guess what? I didn't want to go back anymore! I was so well looked after, because He supplied all my spiritual, emotional and financial needs! Because He was so kind, such a Gentleman, I didn't want to return to where He took me away from.

Then it happened. One morning, while at my mum's in Brazil, I received an international call. It was my earthly husband to tell me he had lost his job he'd had for 22 years! He was made redundant (called a layoff in USA or a "temporary suspension or permanent termination of employment for business reasons, such as when certain positions are no longer necessary or when a business slowdown occurs"). And this proved that the Lord has control of everything... my earthly husband not only lost his job, but he lost it while I was in Brazil! So, according to his words, when he needed me the most I was away...

Yes! I was with My heavenly Husband on a honeymoon!!! The Lord's time is perfect!

While I was still living in a rented bedroom, my earthly husband asked me to come back home several times, but then at the last minute he would change his mind. This was intended to be extremely painful but my Jesus used it every time for my good. At each opportunity, He used it to show me where my heart really was and also to heal me and make me come into His presence. Because of it happening so often, this time when he asked me, it didn't move me at all! I honestly didn't want to move back, but my earthly husband was very firm.

Next fear came, trying to paralyse me... because I didn't have the courage to tell my landlady I was moving out again. I was shaking and very nervous but in the middle of this I heard His voice: "Do not fear, just trust in Me."

"Do not be afraid or discouraged. For the Lord your God is with you wherever you go." (Joshua 1:9b)

"He is not afraid of bad news; his heart is firm, trusting in the Lord" (Psalm 112:7).

Only after listening to His voice and receiving the grace He poured on me, could I give my notice. But the cords of fear were surrounding me in such a way that even though I had given notice one month before moving out, the day before the move, I still didn't have anything packaged! And I do have lots of stuff...

That's because every single day of that month I was praying and asking the Lord to deliver me from my will, asking Him if wasn't His will for me to move back to please come to my rescue because He was better than any man, any husband, any home or children! I continued praising

Him because He cares... "For He knows how weak we are; He remembers we are only dust." (Psalm 103:14)

When I told a like-minded friend that my things weren't ready yet, the day before I was supposed to be moving she said: "You need to trust the Lord, you must remember what the Lord said: Do not fear, just trust in Me! He is your Husband; He will take care of you!!!"

Another verse my heavenly Husband used to reassured me it was Him who was bringing me home was: "And if a believing woman has a husband who is not a believer and he is willing to continue living with her, she must not leave him. For the believing wife brings holiness to her marriage, and the believing husband brings holiness to his marriage" (1 Corinthians 7:13-14).

So, as I said, my Heavenly Husband has been writing a new chapter in this new phase of my journey: He's brought me back to live in my home, but this time, with Him!

Yes, this is a new chapter. Yes, being back is a whole new situation where I need Him even more. As Erin and all the restored ladies say, it will not be easy and they're right. I depend on Him more than ever! Some days my Heavenly Husband sings for me—I literally I wake up with a song in my heart and I know I have to keep singing it because He is ministering to me. Other days He allows trials to come, so it will continue to bring me closer to Him, and other times, He holds me tight in the hot furnace as only a loving Husband would do to burn off any impurities in my heart. There is no way I could live here or could carry on living here without Him, it's impossible, but His grace is sufficient for me, He is all I need.

A new chapter! Yes! Our journey never ends! It doesn't end when we come back home or when a husband moves back home. It doesn't end when our marriages are restored.

It doesn't end when the cords, which are holding us or them are broken. This is a journey of love and discoveries that never ends!

A journey is meant to prepare us for our purpose and destiny: "Look, I am coming soon, bringing my reward with me to repay all people according to their deeds. I am the Alpha and the Omega, the First and the Last, the Beginning and the End."

"Blessed are those who wash their robes. They will be permitted to enter through the gates of the city and eat the fruit from the tree of life. Outside the city are the dogs—the sorcerers, the sexually immoral, the murderers, the idol worshippers, and all who love to live a lie."

"I, Jesus, have sent my angel to give you this message for the churches. I am both the source of David and the heir to his throne. I am the bright morning star."

"The Spirit and the bride say, 'Come.' Let anyone who hears this say, "Come." Let anyone who is thirsty come. Let anyone who desires drink freely from the water of life.

"He who is the faithful witness to all these things says, 'Yes, I am coming soon!'"

Amen! Come, Lord Jesus!" (Revelation 22:12-17, 20)

I want to thank Erin and this ministry for reuniting me and introducing me to my heavenly Husband. And let me say, for any woman who is interested in restoring her marriage, I would highly recommend the *How God Can and Will Restore Your Marriage* book, *A Wise Woman*, *By Word of Their Testimony*, *Workers@Home*, and all other the resources this ministry has to offer—especially the daily lessons offered. It helped me, and will help you restore your relationship, first with your heavenly Husband and then with your earthly husband . And no matter how bad things look, there is nothing impossible with God.

Now I want to use what I've learned to help other women on this same or a similar journey. I've experienced the most terrible things a woman can experience, but the Lord never let me down and He won't let you down either! He was with me in the shadow of death, carrying me in

His arms. And I promise He is there with you now. Just open your heart to Him and let Him heal you and make you His bride.

Thank You for bringing me back home Jesus, this is Your home my Beloved, let Your will be done here. As for me and my house we will serve You! All the glory, honor and praise belong to You alone. I want to be forever with You Author and Finisher of my faith! I love You Jesus.

~ Sarah in Wales is an amazing woman who is like a modern day Sarah "who obeyed Abraham calling him lord." The Lord has helped Sarah carry her very difficult cross to prepare her to minister to other women who are called to go through extremely difficult journeys.

Like What You've Read?
If you've been blessed by this book
By the Word of Their Testimony
(Book 3): Nothing is Impossible With God
Get the WOTT Series available
on EncouragingBookstore.com & Amazon.com

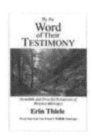 By the Word of Their Testimony (Book 1): Incredible and Powerful Testimonies of Restored Marriages

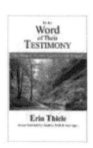 By the Word of Their Testimony (Book 2): No Weapon Formed Against you will Prosper

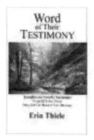 Word of Their Testimony (Book 3): Incredible and Powerful Testimonies of Restored Marriage From Men

Restore Ministries International

POB 830
Ozark, MO 65721
USA

For more help
Please visit one of our Websites:

EncouragingWomen.org

HopeAtLast.com

RestoreMinistries.net

RMIEW.com

AjudaMatrimonial.com (Portuguese)

AyudaMatrimonial.com (Spanish)

Zachranamanzelstva.com (Slovakian)

EncouragingMen.org

Made in the USA
Middletown, DE
28 February 2023

25828912R00128